FROM
THE
Moment
THEY
WERE
BORN

FROM
THE
Moment
THEY
WERE
BORN

★★★★★

CPH
SAINT LOUIS

40 ASSETS FOR GROWING CHRISTIAN TEENS
Edited by Terry K. Dittmer and Mark Sengele

The framework of developmental assets, on which this work is based,
was developed by Search Institute © 1997,
Minneapolis, MN 1-800-888-7828; www.search-institute.org.
Used with permission.

Scripture quotations taken from the HOLY BIBLE, NEW INTERNATIONAL VERSION®.
NIV®.
Copyright © 1973, 1978, 1984 by International Bible Society.
Used by permission of Zondervan Publishing House. All rights reserved.

The development of *From the Moment They Were Born* was made possible
by a grant from Lutheran Brotherhood and was originally produced by the LCMS
Department of Youth Ministry.

Published by Concordia Publishing House
3558 S. Jefferson Avenue, St. Louis, MO 63118–3968
Manufactured in the United States of America

Library of Congress Cataloging-in-Publication Data

1 2 3 4 5 6 7 8 9 10   10 09 08 07 06 05 04 03 02 01

Dedicated to parents who brought teens into this world
and want the best for them, the professional church workers who
work with young people—pastors, teachers,
and professional youth workers—and the countless, dedicated volunteers.
In thanksgiving for all who love the Lord and
strive to help teens as they grow in faith and life.

INTRODUCTION

Several years ago, Search Institute published a list of what they called "developmental assets." The institute determined there were 40 assets, which are qualities or characteristics of life that help build healthy young people. The more assets a young person had in his or her life, the more likely that person would be healthy in body, mind, and spirit. Unfortunately, many youth struggle to identify even a majority of the assets in their lives.

While the 40 assets are not in and of themselves spiritual things, there are obvious spiritual connectors. Based on this assumption, this book of devotional thoughts was developed. Thirty authors have explored spiritual and biblical factors within the list of assets. They have shared stories, experiences, and insights from their perspectives as parents and/or professional and volunteer youth workers. From their wisdom comes this excellent resource for adults who care for and work with youth.

It is interesting how the Lord guides things. Titles are never easy things to identify. What should we call this book? I looked at the titles given to the various articles and at the content of the 40 chapters. It struck me after the entire manuscript had been written, edited, and designed that the first article begins with the story of a mother's love for her newborn child. The last article includes a reference to our future in the Promised Land. Throughout the pages of this book, the cycle of life is the focus as we strive to help young people grow into the people God has in mind. Our writers have covered things from the beginning of life to the end. Thus, we start "from the moment they were born."

May God bless your devotional reading. And may He make you a blessing to the young people with whom you live and work.

Terry K. Dittmer

From the Moment
They Were Born

★★★★★

I praise You because I am fearfully
and wonderfully made;
Your works are wonderful,
I know that full well. My frame was not hidden from
You when I was made in the secret place. When I was woven together
in the depths of the earth, Your eyes saw my unformed body.
All the days ordained for me were written in
Your book before one of them came to be.
Psalm 139:14–16

Asset 1: Family Support
Family life provides high levels of love and support.

Holding that tiny gift in my arms for the first time, I was hooked. From the moment they were born, there was only one option as far as I was concerned—to love them with all of my heart and to be the best mom I could be. As my children have grown, the desire to love them with all my heart and be the best mom for them hasn't changed.

As I quietly creep into their bedroom and watch Ryan and Sean sleep, I am always amazed that these almost six-feet tall young men were once (in my mind, not so long ago) tiny and helpless. Now they are no longer in need of the same mothering. I no longer need to give them baths, make their lunches, tie their shoes, or quietly sing to them as I rock them to sleep. They have grown beyond those needs. But they still need parents who will give them support and encouragement, unconditional love, and the independence to succeed on their own and sometimes fail. God has given these things to each of us as His children, and we, as parents, do the same for the children God has entrusted to our care.

When Sean and Ryan were little, my support included sitting at the kitchen table playing board games, finger painting, reading stories, reviewing spelling words and multiplication tables, or playing outside in the leaves or catching fireflies. It meant holding them close when they had a bad dream or putting a Band-Aid on a scraped knee. I showed my support for them by spending time with them, encouraging them, and letting them know how much they were loved.

Today, my support means proofreading term papers and rehearsing lines for the play, listening when my sons need to vent frustrations or when they want to share something great that has happened. It means cheering them on at volleyball games and wrestling matches, going to drama productions or youth group outings. My support is demonstrated when I take Ryan driving, encourage him as his skills improve; and try not to grab the wheel, step on the brakes, or scream in terror when he doesn't do what I think he should. As parents, we show support when Tim runs in one direction with Sean while I go in another with Ryan. It means being there for our sons when they need us.

We want what is best for our children, but sometimes they want things that might not be best. It is difficult to allow young people the independence to make mistakes, but part of supporting and loving our sons is trusting that they have good heads on their shoulders and that they will make use of them. Each day we pray that God will watch over them. He loved them first and He knows what is best for them.

Prayer: Father in heaven, we thank You for these children You have entrusted to our care. Forgive us when we make mistakes and help us to forgive ourselves. Give us the patience and strength we need to guide our children as they grow, and continue to help us seek Your guidance to do Your will. Grant us little joys amid the chaos, and remind us that we need to reaffirm daily to our children that they have our support and unconditional love. Hold us close to You, and fill us with Your love. In Jesus' name we pray. Amen.

Elizabeth McAdams

Be There!

Fix these words of Mine in your hearts and minds; tie them as symbols on your hands and bind them on your foreheads. Teach them to your children, talking about them when you sit at home and when you walk along the road, when you lie down and when you get up.
Deuteronomy 11:18–19

ASSET 2: POSITIVE FAMILY COMMUNICATION
Young person and his or her parent(s) communicate positively, and young person is willing to seek advice and counsel from parent(s).

One of the best gifts both parents and young people can give to each other is to "Be there!" To be available to talk and listen, share and pray, with one another is truly a privilege. Some have called it a "ministry of presence."

Parents and youth can be there for each other because the Lord is already there—right where they are! We are there for each other because God's promise continues to echo in our ears and lives—"I am with you always, to the very end of the age" (Matthew 28:20).

In today's hectic and fast-paced lifestyle, it can be difficult to find time and take time for parents and youth to be there for each other. That is our challenge as parents, young people, volunteer youth workers, and professional church workers. One way to help young people sense the importance of spending time with family members is to model in our own lives the importance of spending time with our own family members!

Many years ago, the Bimler family tried various ways to communicate intentionally with one another. For example, we tried "strength bombardment" exercises during mealtime when our kids were young. Every member of the family had to say something positive about every other family member during dinner. We wouldn't leave the table until these positive words were shared. At times it seemed like we spent two hours at dinner, but it was a helpful exercise to encourage each of us to speak positively, look forgivingly, and practice being there for one another.

The encouraging thing about being there for others is that the Lord is already there for us! Even when we fail to recognize His presence, even when we fail to spend time together with our family, God continues to forgive us and to provide us with more opportunities to share His forgiveness and love with those closest to us.

Practice being there with people close to you this week. Being there in the name of the Lord is a gift that the Lord has given to each of us. Blessings to you as you give away this gift to those closest to you and as you help others give the gift of being there to their family and friends.

Prayer: Lord, thanks for being there for us. Thanks for being on the cross and for being with us as our resurrected Lord each day. Bless us, our families, and the youth and parents around us as together we serve and share You. Amen.

Richard Bimler

HE COULD HAVE BLOWN ME OFF,
BUT HE DIDN'T

★★★★★

Don't let anyone look down on you because you are young,
but set an example for the believers in speech, in life, in love,
in faith and in purity. Until I come, devote yourself to the public
reading of Scripture, to preaching and to teaching.
1 Timothy 4:12–13

ASSET 3: OTHER ADULT RELATIONSHIPS
Young person receives support from three or more non-parent adults.

Growing up, I was blessed to have a variety of adults who invested their time and energy in me. Teachers, pastors, youth workers, neighbors, aunts, and uncles—all of these people helped to encourage, teach, and guide me.

God blessed me through these people. He provided me with adults who genuinely cared about me and wanted to encourage me in my endeavors. Our church had a group of adults who truly believed in the youth of our congregation and spent time engaging us in Bible study and fellowship, encouraging us to serve God in our church and community. They helped us to discover who we were and gave us opportunities to grow.

I believe my love for God and desire to serve His young people is deeply rooted in the experiences I had growing up in my church. I was given opportunities to develop as a leader. I also was given the opportunity to make mistakes and learn from them. These people shared their joy of serving God with me. Many of them are still important in my life. Some, however, have gone home to serve God face-to-face. Their impact on me will remain forever.

One memorable experience came when I was a high school junior.

I was given the opportunity to participate in a leadership training weekend sponsored by our denominational district. What an uplifting experience! I spent the weekend with other youth and committed adults who wanted to help us grow in our faith and our leadership skills. Among the adults was Pastor Bill Ameiss. He was wonderful. He took the time to listen to us and talk with us. He encouraged us to stay in contact with him. We knew his love for God and his concern for us were real.

The weekend ended, and we left filled with excitement and enthusiasm. Arriving home, all the joy from the weekend turned to sadness with the news that our pastor had died that morning. I was devastated. How could this happen? He was one of those adults who believed in the youth of our congregation—he was a friend. I called Bill, and even though I was just a youth, he took the time to listen to me and comfort me. My feelings mattered; my loss was real. He could have blown me off, but he didn't.

A few years later, our paths crossed again, this time when I was a college student. I was in a class he was teaching. He was the same caring man I had first encountered in high school. Fast forward many years, and as an adult I am still blessed to have contact with Bill. He still radiates God's love, and his commitment and love for youth is still evident. He was in Atlanta recently for a national youth gathering and spent time talking, listening, and interacting with the youth from the congregation I now serve. What a blessing he continues to be.

Now I serve on our denominational district's youth board, and I feel especially blessed to be able to give back to God's people for all they did for me as a youth. God placed some wonderful adults in my life to serve as incredible role models. What a gift these people have been and continue to be in my life.

As you interact with young people in your congregation, you touch their lives. You help to mold who they are. When you listen to their concerns, their hopes, and their dreams, you affirm that they have value and importance. By investing your time and energy in them, your love of Jesus is reflected in the love you show to His children. What a blessing you are!

Prayer: Gracious Father, thank You for the blessings You have given to the youth of our church through caring adults who take the time to love them, work with them, encourage them, and nurture them. Bless the efforts of these parents and workers, and send Your Spirit to encourage them in their efforts. Let them never forget the special calling You have given them to love and serve Your children. In Jesus' name we pray. Amen.

Elizabeth McAdams

A Hug on the Back Porch

Jesus sat down opposite the place where the offerings were put and watched the crowd putting their money into the temple treasury. Many rich people threw in large amounts. But a poor widow came and put in two very small copper coins, worth only a fraction of a penny. Calling His disciples to Him, Jesus said, "I tell you the truth, this poor widow has put more into the treasury than all the others. They all gave out of their wealth; but she, out of her poverty, put in everything—all she had to live on."
Mark 12:41–44

Asset 4: Caring Neighborhood
Young person experiences caring neighbors.

Because of His own humble circumstances, Jesus could, no doubt, identify with the widow. He once remarked, "Foxes have holes and birds of the air have nests, but the Son of Man has no place to lay His head" (Matthew 8:20).

Although this story was written for us thousands of years ago, such widows can still be found in our world today. Hilda was one example. She lived two farms down from mine when I was a young boy. We lived in a small farming community in southern Missouri. It was a wonderful place known for its country fairs, a farm equipment museum, and tail fish dinners with real German potato salad. No one lived in big fancy houses. We didn't drive brand-new shiny cars. There was nothing exciting to do, nothing exciting to see. Hilda's farmhouse was no exception. Some chickens here, some cattle there, and the smell of manure everywhere.

Our family would visit Hilda frequently. After her husband died, we were a source of friendship and conversation.

I hated going to Hilda's home.

As I would crawl out of the car, the expression on my face said a thousand words. "Here we go again," I would mumble under my breath. Hilda would wait at the back door with arms extended, looking for a hearty hug. I hated those hugs!

My family knew that Hilda was excited to see us because her chubby face, decorated with long whiskers sprouting from her chin and lip, would be stretched with a smile from ear to ear. Her hair hadn't been washed that morning. In fact, I don't know if it was washed the morning before.

We'd start our visit with Hilda over dinner. These meals did not consist of pizza, hamburgers, french fries, or ice cream, like most children crave. Instead, we sat down to a meal of pork sausage patties, sweet and sour pickles, and toast. Sure, Hilda was less than wealthy, but couldn't she splurge a little when we visited? The beverages were no different. We had the choice of water or root beer. I would have loved a tall glass of milk, but milk was too expensive for someone who lived alone. Milk was used only in coffee and baking—nothing more. Because the water tasted and looked like it came straight from the Mississippi River, we usually settled for root beer. Hilda always had root beer. It was the cheapest soda at the market.

Weren't we worth more to her?

Hilda was no authority on toys for children either. The toys she owned consisted of metal tractors, plastic farm animals, dominos, and checkers. As you can imagine, her toys did not keep my attention for long.

I also remember our annual Christmas visit to Hilda's home. The tree was artificial, and gaudy trinkets hung from the feeble branches. I usually received socks or gloves as gifts. Once in a great while I got a toy. I once received an olive green plastic helicopter. Big deal! Who cares? When are we going home?

Things didn't change as I grew older. As Hilda aged, the responsibilities of the farm fell on the shoulders of my father and me. We would spend our Saturdays mowing the lawn, hoeing the garden, filling feed sacks with grain, and cleaning the house. Other kids my age could have charged twenty, thirty, even forty bucks for all these services—but I got a root beer and a smile. I wasted my entire Saturday, working my fingers to the bone, for a stinking root beer. Didn't Hilda have more to offer? Couldn't she give me a little more than this?

Now I am older, and as I read about the widow's mite, I can't help but feel ashamed as I remember Hilda. She offered so much—everything she had. The best that she had to offer, she offered with no reservation.

Couldn't we appreciate the love that she gave us, knowing that someone in this world longed for the love and happiness that Hilda had to offer? Couldn't we appreciate the food that graced our table, knowing that some people go days without food to eat? Couldn't we appreciate the old toys in the closet, knowing that the eyes of a homeless child would have twinkled on Christmas morning if only one of those gifts would have been under the tree?

How could I have been so callous? How could I have been so cold?

Hilda now lives in a nursing home. When we visit, she apologizes for not being able to offer us coffee or a root beer. I humbly say, "That's okay. I had something to drink before we came to visit."

From now on, I'll always accept a good-bye kiss and hug from Hilda, not knowing whether it will be my last. Hilda is old, and she won't be on this earth forever. I long to visit that old farmhouse in southern Missouri. I don't know who is living there or even if it is still standing, but I long for the memories of a small boy and an old woman hugging on the back porch.

Prayer: Thank You, Lord, for the many blessings that have been given to me. Help me to appreciate them as a gift from You. Help me use my gifts to support the ministry of the church with young people. In Jesus' name. Amen.

Jeffrey Meinz

FRIGID? TEMPERATE? HOT?

★★★★★

Read Hebrews 1:1–12

ASSET 5: CARING SCHOOL CLIMATE
School provides a caring, encouraging environment.

Your contact with young people familiarizes you with the schools they attend. Has much changed since you were their age? Think back. What was your best experience in school? Your worst? What was the school climate—frigid, temperate, hot?

What happens in school affects young people in many ways. These influences commonly bounce between positive and negative during the course of a day or a week. A "caring" school environment may seem caring one day and cruel the next. In fact, instead of talking about school climate, perhaps we should talk about school weather!

It's true, of course, that school climate isn't nearly as changeable as the kids who live in it. As variable as their experiences and emotions are, one thing remains constant, as the writer to the Hebrews says about Jesus, "But You remain the same, and Your years will never end" (Hebrews 1:12b).

Eventually the worst moments of high school will end. So will the best! As you live with and interact with young people, your challenge is to keep them focused on the unchangeable love that Jesus has for them. In reminding them, you will remember it too.

You've probably developed empathy with your children or with the members of your church's youth group. You hurt when they hurt, you laugh when they laugh, and sometimes you're not sure what to do. While it seems that influencing the existence of a caring school climate lies beyond your control, you and your kids certainly feel its affects.

You hear much about an uncaring school climate—teacher strikes, budget and program cuts, self-centered teachers, and friends who aren't always friends. I also hope you hear about the good times—the new friend, a great basketball game, and teachers who go beyond expectations to nurture students. Undoubtedly, you'll hear things that frighten you, and you'll be a terrified spectator, watching spiritual battles fought over the souls of your kids. Satan loves young people—they're so vulnerable, and they don't even know it.

Young people might think that God never went to school. And when Jesus attended, He ended up in the enviable position of teaching the teachers. Yet God is always in school, despite laws to the contrary. Jesus said, "I am with you always, to the very end of the age" (Matthew 28:20). He is with your kids, so perhaps you can relax a bit, though battles rage for their eternal welfare. You see, God is doing for them what He did for you. By the power of the Holy Spirit working through the Word, He has kept you faithful and fruitful. Otherwise you wouldn't be doing what you're doing. After all, who in their right mind parents teenagers or volunteers to work with the youth group? Don't fret. Your mind is all right. God made it that way, and He wants to do the same for your kids.

Perhaps it's helpful to remember that we can't separate any one element of living from the whole that we call spiritual life. The kids in school, whatever the climate, are still living within their spiritual lives. Your children or the members of your youth group may seem more spiritual than junior high or high school hallways, but it's just another facet of spiritual life. And that's good news! Regardless of whether a local school's climate is caring or indifferent, loving or laced with evil, your kids have the Christian advantage. That advantage lies not in how the kids act or what decisions they make, but their advantage is a Savior who cares for them more than any school can. Their advantage lies in what God has done for them—and you—through Jesus Christ. Knowing that, you can lead your kids to be rays of Christian light that warm the climate of any school.

In what God-pleasing ways can you help kids maximize or positively influence the climate that, in turn, influences them? At the very least, how can you protect them if the climate is harsh and menacing? Here are some ideas:

Pray. Because this activity is so easy, you might take prayer lightly. But God doesn't. When you talk, He listens! When you place your kids in His loving hands, He will mold their lives, caring for them according to His will. Psalm 9:10 says, "Those who know Your name will trust in You, for You, LORD, have never forsaken those who seek You."

Listen. Wide-open ears are twice as effective as a wide-open mouth. Make it possible for kids to trust you and know that, as God's servant, you also serve them. When you don't know answers, say so. Then search God's Word (a good topical Bible helps) for insights. He's been around schools long enough to know all the problems. And He's wise enough to provide the best solutions.

Speak. The Gospel mostly. One big temptation is to lecture or advise (*a.k.a.* preach). Speaking the Gospel lets kids know that God loves them even when their teachers or classmates don't. The Gospel tells kids that in trusting Jesus with their lives, there is less sting when their lives become like jammed lockers. The Gospel assures them that even if they die, God has a solution for that too.

Be assured of this: When you walk and talk with God, He'll gladly accompany you into any climate—school, family, workplace. Speaking of you, Jesus has told God, "This is one of Your kids."

Prayer: Thank You, dear Father, for making me Your own and for giving me the privilege of serving Your other kids. Bless our schools. Give them caring, Christian teachers and students who seek to serve You. Bring them a climate warmed by Your Son. In Jesus' name. Amen.

Ed Grube

"Homework Tonight?"

★★★★★

Recalling your tears, I long to see you, so that I may be filled with joy.
I have been reminded of your sincere faith, which first lived in your
grandmother Lois and in your mother Eunice and, I am persuaded,
now lives in you also. For this reason I remind you to fan into flame
the gift of God, which is in you through the laying on of my hands.
For God did not give us a spirit of timidity, but a spirit of power, of
love and of self-discipline.
2 Timothy 1:4–7

Asset 6: Parent Involvement in Schooling
Parent(s) are actively involved in helping young person succeed in school.

Timothy was sitting on the front steps of his house, taking a break from his homework. He was thinking about the essay he had to write when his friends came by and called for him to join them in a kickball game down at the local park.

He called into the house where his mother, Eunice, and his grandmother Lois were busy in the kitchen preparing the meal. "Hey, Mom, can I go with Phygelus and Hermogenes to the park to play kickball? I promise to write the essay as soon as I get back. Please, may I go?"

"I suppose," his mother answered back. "But be back in an hour for supper. And after supper you will need to finish up the essay assignment."

Such an exchange could have taken place between Timothy and his mother, Eunice. Apparently both Eunice and Timothy's grandmother Lois were involved in the education of young Timothy. Paul relates in 2 Timothy 1:5 that faith "first lived in your grandmother Lois and in your mother Eunice and I am persuaded, now lives in you also."

We are told in Acts 16:1 that Eunice was a Jewish Christian and that Lois apparently had become a Christian as well. The only thing we know about Timothy's father is that he was Greek and probably not a Christian.

The Bible does not say much about Timothy's formal training, so we do not know if he was taught at home or in a school. We are told that he was a native of Lystra and that from childhood he had been taught about the Old Testament. Timothy came to faith by the Holy Spirit working through the power of the Gospel. That Gospel was, no doubt, taught and modeled by his mother and grandmother in his young life. Paul also became an influence in this young pastor's life. We can assume that Timothy probably learned at the feet of Paul as they traveled together on the missionary journeys.

The story of Timothy's family sounds surprisingly similar to that of some modern families. As a Christian school principal, I see a variety of families—traditional families, one-parent families, blended families, families with joint custody, extended families, and even families similar to Timothy's in which one parent seems to have great influence over a child's faith life.

A key to academic success as well as success in spiritual matters seems to be a parent's support and involvement in helping that child grow. A child will succeed when one or both parents are there to work with and underscore the learning that happens in school.

This can happen in a variety of ways. First, communication with the student's teacher(s) is important in understanding what is happening in the classroom. Don't be afraid to ask questions—especially if there is a story that comes home from school that does not sound quite right. There are always two sides to any story. When communicating, show support and respect for the teacher, especially in front of your children. Second, support your students in their schoolwork. Establish a time for homework, and be there for your children when they get "stuck" or have questions. Help them to be organized with their schoolwork. Learning does take effort. Third, follow up on suggestions that the teacher may make to help a student. It's important that actions at school and home are in harmony with each other.

Students are confused by messages that are different at school and at home. Fourth, make learning active and fun. Read to your children when they are young, and look for chances to help them expand their horizons with learning games, family outings to museums, vacations, walks, and other "teachable moments." Reinforce the lessons that are taught in school. Fifth, model good learning approaches for your child. You are never too old to learn something new. Develop a new hobby. Pick up a new interest. Especially display the love of learning about God's Word by attending Bible class and worshiping on a weekly basis. Children will learn about the love of learning from the model that is set by you as a parent.

The Holy Spirit gave Timothy faith through which he took hold of the benefits of God's grace. As a parent and a grandparent, Eunice and Lois were there for Timothy. As a teacher, Paul was like a father for this preacher. They all supported the education of this one boy who grew up to know God's spiritual truths and to become a leader in God's kingdom.

> **Prayer:** Dear Father, please be with teachers and parents as they work together for the education of Your children. Help them to communicate in ways that please You and help the student. Allow them to be models of Christian learning for the children who learn from them. Forgive us for the times when we are less than perfect in that communication and modeling. In Jesus' name we pray. Amen.

Dave Ingwersen

VALUED?

*These commandments that I give you today are to be upon your
hearts. Impress them on your children. Talk about them when you sit
at home and when you walk along the road,
when you lie down and when you get up.*
Deuteronomy 6:6–7

ASSET 7: COMMUNITY VALUES YOUTH
Young person perceives that adults in the community value youth.

I went as soon as I heard. One of our teens had been riding his bike
when a delivery truck broadsided him. Some of my worst fears were realized when I was allowed into the ICU. I would not have recognized him
except his mom was standing beside him. So many tubes, a swollen face,
and medical personnel everywhere—it seemed almost surreal.

What I remember most from all the visits and prayers in the following weeks as God slowly unfolded a healing miracle was a conversation with that young man after he had returned home. He told me
that he remembered me speaking to him as he slipped in and out of
consciousness those first few days. He especially remembered me
because I spoke *to* him. Others, even members of his family, usually
spoke to one another about him.

He had felt comfort and reassurance that he would make it, that he
was still a human being, because I spoke to him and not about him
when others seemed to assume he was unconscious and unable to hear.
People are valued, reassured, and strengthened when they are included, when they are spoken to and not about.

I asked students in one of my classes what made them feel valued
and special in our community and in our church. These are some of their
responses:

• When someone pays a compliment I don't expect.

• When an adult listens to my opinion and takes me seriously.

- When someone guides me through an awkward moment so I look okay.

- When I have a place to go.

- When we have options. When pressed to explain, this included Little League, soccer, lacrosse, and many other sport choices but also a place to "hang out." Our urban middleclass neighborhood has many clubs, but they are for young adults of drinking age—and that's what happens there.

- When we are part of church (meaning services) like reading and acolyting. Well, that one did my heart good!

Youth are like people of any age. They want to be valued in all the ways you as an adult want to be valued. They like to hear about how they are doing well. They like to look good and be guided to do so. They want to be included and not considered as an afterthought.

In the Old Testament and in our Savior we have the example and expectation to treat youth with respect—something we often have failed to do. God did not mean for youth to be second-class citizens in the kingdom of God. Young people are a treasure to be nurtured and valued. There are many ways for us to let them know we do value them—but we cannot leave it to chance.

As our Savior died for all, as He sent us to "all nations," as we are called by name in our Baptism, may we who live with and work with young people help them to see the value they have in God's eyes.

Prayer: Lord God our Father, as a loving Father and creator of all, You value all You have made. Teach us, use us, so our words and works may speak of Your value of our youth. May we value them as individuals so they may see the reflection of Your unconditional love in us. Through the same Jesus who took young ones in His arms. Amen.

Harold Therwanger

The Giant's about to
Lose His Head

★★★★★

Read 1 Samuel 17

Asset 8: Youth as Resources
Young person is given useful roles in the community.

"He what?" the king roared.

"He's willing to take on the giant, your majesty."

"Take on the giant?!? Take *on* the giant!?! What do you mean, 'Take on the giant'?"

"Well, he heard the giant out on the field this morning, jeering and making fun of us. And he asked 'Why doesn't somebody do something?' When nobody would answer him, he just up and said, 'Well, I'll do it then!' "

"How old is he?" the king asked incredulously.

"Oh, maybe 13, 14 at the most. Kind of a scrawny kid."

"And where did he come from?"

"Well, he brought up some grain and cheese for his brothers who are all in the army."

"Well, that certainly sounds like something a 14-year-old can do. But fight the giant?" And the king collapsed on his throne. "What makes him think he can fight the giant?"

"Don't know, your majesty. But he does keep mumbling something about he can do it in the name of the Lord."

"Bring him to me," the king said, exasperated.

A bit later.

"So, boy, what makes you think you're a giant killer?"

"Well, God saw to it that I could do in a bear and I had no problem with a lion. So what's a guy who's grown a little too big for his britches going to do to me? The Lord will deliver me."

"I don't know. You're a nice-looking kid, but kind of scrawny. How 'bout trying out my armor?"

"I don't think this is gonna work. I'm draggin' your sword on the ground. Thanks for offering, but I can't do it with this stuff. Just let me go, and God will take care of the big guy."

A little later.

"He used what?"

"Well, he took five stones he picked up out of the creek bed. But he only used one. Shot the guy on the first shot—with his slingshot."

"A what?"

"It was amazing! Right between the eyes. Then he ran up to the guy, pulled out the giant's own sword, and chopped of his head right in front of all of us and the Philistines. And the Philistines got so excited, they ran off screaming and yelling. It was great!"

"Great?!? A kid. A kid!" King Saul sat down with a sigh. "A kid."

Kids are supposed to know their place. They're not supposed to be able to do great things. They are, after all, just kids. Giants aren't their business. Basketball and flute lessons and video games—that's the stuff kids are supposed to do.

It's a shame so many people feel that way. Kids have extraordinary gifts, energy, enthusiasm, and insight. They're not afraid to try new things, to change things, to take on giants, as it were. Just because they're 13 or 14 or 17 doesn't mean they don't have something to offer. It doesn't mean they can't help. It doesn't mean they won't help. It's mostly a matter of helping to channel their gifts and drive in service to God's kingdom.

We have to get past our stereotypes. It is often in our best interest to listen to young people when they say, "I'll take care of it. No problem." And despite our best inclinations, sometimes we have to let them do it their way even if it means letting them use a toy. 'Cause you know what?

The giant's about to lose his head.

Prayer: Lord, thanks for the blessings of young people. Thanks for the gifts You have given to them. Thanks for their creativity and energy. Thanks for the questions they ask, for their interest and curiosity. I'm sorry that sometimes I miss the people they are, the gifts they have, and say, "Hey, he's only a kid. She's too young. What can they possibly have to offer?" Help me to see and love the kids You have given as resources to Your Church, to discover with them their gifts and abilities, to encourage them, and to get out of their way so they can do it. Help me to remember that they can do and they will. In Jesus' name. Amen.

Terry K. Dittmer

SIMPLE ACTS OF SERVICE

★★★★★

*This service that you perform is not only supplying
the needs of God's people but is also overflowing in many
expressions of thanks to God. Because of the service by which you have
proved yourselves, men will praise God for the obedience that
accompanies your confession of the gospel of Christ, and for your
generosity in sharing with them and with everyone else.*
2 Corinthians 9:12–13

ASSET 9: SERVICE TO OTHERS
Young person serves in the community one hour or more per week.

*We make a living by what we get, but we make a
life by what we give.*—Winston Churchill

Somewhere early on in the blur of my high school years, Nadine Brandt asked me to lead crafts for a special education class she conducted at my church. Many of these mentally handicapped adults came from a nearby group home and joined the members of our congregation each Sunday for worship before attending their own Sunday school class.

I agreed to lead crafts. For almost two years, I spent an hour each Sunday morning with this group of folks. It really was a kick. They loved singing the songs, eating donuts, listening to the stories, repeating the key words they knew, and, of course, getting their fingers really full of glue and glitter or whatever else was the basis of the craft activity that week.

During that time, I became really good at figuring out a gazillion craft projects you could do with paper plates. I learned how to get Eddie, a 65-year-old man with the heart of a 4-year-old, to laugh and smile his huge, make-everybody-else-in-the-room-catch-it smile. I also learned that I really enjoyed spending time with this group of special individuals.

I can't imagine that Nadine Brandt had any great plan in mind when she asked me to lead crafts. I think she didn't know what to do with all those paper plates. She may even be surprised to know it made such an impact on my life. Pretty soon I was leading games when our youth group got together and teaching a vacation Bible school class for first-graders. My pastor mentioned one Sunday that I should think about becoming a Christian teacher. I enrolled at one of our denomination's colleges, which offered many options, including teaching and special education degrees.

It really is amazing how God used that one hour in my life each week—a simple servant opportunity—to sow His seeds of lifelong servanthood.

Kind of makes you think, doesn't it, especially about the youth in your life. God has plans for all of them, plans that you may never know or see come to fulfillment in the immediate future. But the plan that God has for all of us is that we daily reach out to others with Christlike care and the message of His love for all people.

Simple acts of service go a long way. So do you have any paper plates lying around that you don't know what to do with?

Prayer: Dear Lord Jesus, You present so many servant opportunities to me each day. Make me mindful of these opportunities to share Your love in ways that may be simple but meaningful to many. Help me to model a love of service with the youth around me. Send Your Spirit to encourage their service to You so they are able to leave behind "fingerprints of faith" in Your name. In Jesus' name we serve and pray. Amen.

Julie Johnston

They'll Be Okay!

I will lie down and sleep in peace, for You alone,
O LORD, make me dwell in safety.
Psalm 4:8

ASSET 10: SAFETY
Young person feels safe at home, school, and in the neighborhood.

During my numerous years in youth ministry, the annual summer trip to a theme park became part of the routine. This event was also the first trip that the new youth group members were allowed to attend. It was popular with these just-turned teenagers.

Each year I met with parents and tried to reassure them of the safety measures and level of supervision from the park staff. I explained to them how the adult leaders met with the youth on a regular basis to make sure that everyone was doing well, eating something, and remembering to put on sunblock. I also reminded the parents that we had chartered a bus so we did not have to arrange transportation with parent drivers. With these reassurances, most parents happily signed up their child for the trip.

One of the great attractions to theme park rides is the adrenaline-pumping sensation of being in a dangerous situation. The best rides give this illusion while really providing for complete passenger safety. If the number of injuries occurred that your imagination or urban legend would have you believe, the ride would have been shut down long ago. You are safer on rides than you are on the road to the park. Little did I know how one particular summer trip would prove that fact.

After an early morning departure from home, our bus was sitting in snarled Chicago rush hour traffic. Suddenly the bus was rear-ended by a fully loaded semi. Everything loose came flying to the front of the bus, including Walkmans, Gameboys, and lunches. One of our chaperones that day was a father who worked as an ER physician. In the moments that followed the accident, we determined that no one had been seriously injured. Sitting in a crippled bus, we offered a prayer of thanks to God for our safety. I offered my own prayer of thanks that God sent along the right chaperones that day.

Within minutes, the state police arrived and moved our battered bus to the side of the highway. The accident had occurred under one of the overpass Oasis restaurants, so we moved the youth to a safer location to await the arrival of a replacement bus. In the end, we arrived at the park only about two hours behind schedule. We enjoyed a beautiful day at the park and returned home without any further adventures. The youth said that the bus trip turned out to be the wildest ride of the day.

The events of that day have reminded me of how very important safety is for young people. While we enjoy the brief thrill and sensation of riding on an amusement park ride, we do so knowing we are not in any real danger. It is when we are going about our daily routine that we face real threats to our safety.

Throughout the Old Testament, God reassured the children of Israel of His promise of a land of their own where they could dwell in safety. But even that land would pass away, and one day God would take all His followers to be with Him, safe for all eternity.

> "I will place shepherds over them who will tend them, and they will no longer be afraid or terrified, nor will any be missing," declares the LORD. "The days are coming," declares the LORD, "when I will raise up to David a righteous Branch, a King who will reign wisely and do what is just and right in the land. In His days Judah will be saved and Israel will live in safety. This is the name by which He will be called: The LORD our righteousness." (Jeremiah 23:4–6)

God knew how important it was for His chosen people to feel safe in their new homeland. It is no different for young people today. In a world that threatens from all sides, it is important that we help to provide a place of refuge and safety. It may be in our churches, youth programs, or homes. Wherever it is, we can trust in the Lord to provide.

Prayer: Lord, You alone cause us to dwell in safety. Help us to carry out Your will in our lives. Give us the strength, encouragement, and resources that we need to provide for the safety of the young people with whom we live and work. Thank You for Your promise of eternal safety with You in heaven. In Jesus' name. Amen.

Mark Sengele

Boundaries Are a Good Thing!

★★★★★

*He must manage his own family well and see that
his children obey him with proper respect.*
1 Timothy 3:4

*Blessed is the man who fears the LORD, who finds great delight in
His commands. His children will be mighty in the land;
the generation of the upright will be blessed.*
Psalm 112:1–2

ASSET 11: FAMILY BOUNDARIES
*Family has clear rules and consequences and monitors the young
person's whereabouts.*

When I asked a group of youth at our church what they thought
about family boundaries and what they wanted to tell adults about
boundaries, some of their responses surprised me. Just when you think
they have no clue or are the most irresponsible people alive, youth
impress you! And that is what boundaries are all about. Often, we get
caught up in trying to be the perfect parent or volunteer, and we forget whom we are working with—the children of the *only* perfect parent, God. They do have a clue about boundaries. They want boundaries. They know what good family boundaries look like.

Family boundaries are good so the family members can
respect each other.—Tuesday

Each person must play a part in the family guidelines and
morals.—Jessica

Family boundaries need to be based on honesty and
trust.—Andrea

I think if more families had boundaries, there wouldn't be
as many problems with teens.—Ricky

Family boundaries directly relate to "Honor your father and your mother."—Andrew

God is in the center of a family with boundaries.—Matt

Family boundaries. Here's what my eighth- and ninth-grade Bible class kids would like adults to know!

Parents must set the rules because they have the wisdom, experience, and knowledge to set good age-appropriate rules to keep us safe.

The only reason we will abide by the rules is if we respect you and them.

We should know about and agree upon consequences before a rule is broken.

We want to keep the lines of communication open. Give us a chance to talk about things and give our input.

In 1 Timothy, parents are clearly instructed to be in charge of their families. We are to be the ones to set the directions and guidelines. But how do we do this? The best family to pattern our family after is God's family. We can base our boundaries on God's rules. Boundaries based on our merit or reason are often questioned and easily picked apart. But boundaries based on God's reason are solid rocks upon which to build. Pray for His wisdom!

May we also echo Paul in 2 Corinthians 7:4 in our parenting. Our youth not only feel our love through family boundaries, but as we say, "I have great confidence in you; I take great pride in you. I am greatly encouraged; in all our troubles my *joy knows no bounds*" (emphasis added). This truly is the message that God the Father has given us through His mercy and grace brought by Jesus' death and resurrection.

Godly parenting reaps blessings for our kids. By the grace of God, our kids have great things in store for them, a truth the Psalmist celebrates in Psalm 112:1–2.

Prayer: Lord, help us raise our children according to Your truth and grace through Jesus Christ, our Lord. Amen.

Mary Lightbody

RULES, RULES, RULES!

The fear of the LORD is the beginning of knowledge, but fools despise wisdom and discipline. Listen, my son, to your father's instruction and do not forsake your mother's teaching. They will be a garland to grace your head and a chain to adorn your neck.
Proverbs 1:7–9

ASSET 12: SCHOOL BOUNDARIES
School provides clear rules and consequences.

Rules, rules, RULES! They're everywhere. You can't escape them. Play a game—there are rules. Drive a car—there are rules. God gave Moses and the children of Israel rules too. He gives them to us as well. We have rules to give us parameters within which to live. Without rules, we would have chaos.

At the Christian day school my children attended, each new school year began with home visits from their teachers. During the visits, we would discuss the teacher's expectations for the class. The teacher would explain the rules for behavior in class, what was expected, and what we could expect as well. We would review the student handbook, noting any changes or additions.

This was a good way to begin. Everyone went into the school year with clear expectations because the rules and the consequences for disobeying the rules were clearly spelled out. There were no surprises. Better still, the rules and expectations were enforced. They weren't just suggested dos and don'ts—they were clear expectations.

Over the years, people tried to bend the rules, push the envelope of the dress code, or find loopholes to a particular expectation. In light of the events at Columbine High School in Colorado, I have a renewed sense of gratitude and respect for the student handbook and its content. In talking with my sons about the events at Columbine, I think they have a newfound understanding of why some of these rules are necessary.

One year at our school, a student threatened to bring a gun to school and kill a younger student. The child that was threatened was frightened to tears, but an adult heard the exchange and acted on it, assuming it was not a case of "kids being kids." Could this child have had access to a parent's gun and brought the weapon to school and hurt someone? It could have happened, but the student who had made the threat was temporarily removed from school, and his parents decided it was best to transfer him. Sadly, because of the decision to transfer the child, there was little opportunity to witness the healing power of forgiveness, which we as Christians have.

A second incident occurred not long after this in which a student threatened bodily harm to another. Disciplinary action was taken and the student eventually returned to class. Following this incident, the principal visited every classroom and discussed both events. He explained that the school would not tolerate this sort of behavior. There would be serious consequences, even if you were just kidding around. He reassured the students that the school was a place where they could feel safe and that if someone made them feel unsafe, they should tell him or a teacher right away.

A detailed explanation of both incidents also was distributed to parents. We were told that the school would have zero tolerance concerning acts or even threats of violence toward others. This sort of behavior was not acceptable and would not be allowed. We were encouraged to talk to our kids, check out what they were viewing on TV, discover what video games they were playing, and learn what music they listened to. We were encouraged to be actively involved in what our kids were doing. We should have been reminded to pray for wisdom and guidance, not only for ourselves as parents, but also for those who teach. Their task is not easy, especially in our current society.

Funny, many people probably think "This sort of thing can't happen at *my* school." I didn't think it was possible at mine. But it does happen more often than we would like to admit. Truth is, we live in a world filled with sin. Because of that sin, rules become a necessary part of our lives. When a rule is enforced, however, some parents decide the rule is for everyone else and not their kids. They don't back the school, and their lack of support reinforces the idea that not following the rules is acceptable.

The establishment of clear rules and consequences provides a comfort zone for our children. It also provides a comfort zone for us as parents. If there are no rules, no expectations, how can learning and growing take place? It can't. And there are great blessings to be had. Look again at Proverbs 1:7–9: "The fear of the LORD is the beginning of knowledge, but fools despise wisdom and discipline. Listen, my son, to your father's instruction and do not forsake your mother's teaching. They will be a garland to grace your head and a chain to adorn your neck."

I am thankful for the boundaries that the school provides for my kids. I'm thankful for the teachers and youth workers who make my children accountable for their actions. It isn't always easy to be the "enforcer." More often than not, when you act in that role, you hear a lot of complaining and criticism and very little, if any, thanks. You need to know that there are people who are grateful for the work you do. God has given you the responsibility to be mirrors for the young people entrusted to you. What an awesome responsibility and an incredible blessing!

Prayer: Heavenly Father, thank You for schools that give us clear rules and consequences and people who enforce them to provide us with a safe environment in which to learn. Bless the efforts of these special servants, and give them a loving heart to deal compassionately with Your children as they witness Your love through their actions. In Jesus' name. Amen.

Elizabeth McAdams

You Never Know Who's Watching

★★★★★

Therefore each of you must put off falsehood and speak truthfully to
his neighbor, for we are all members of one body.
Be kind and compassionate to one another, forgiving each other,
just as in Christ God forgave you.
Ephesians 4:25, 32

Asset 13: Neighborhood Boundaries
Neighbors take responsibility for
monitoring young person's behavior.

I grew up in a *Leave It to Beaver* rural neighborhood in western Maryland during the late '50s and early '60s. There were 19 homes in my little village. They were all on my paper route, so I encountered most of my neighbors on a daily basis and knew everyone by name.

At Halloween the traditional trick or treat ritual took several hours because our little band of costumed children would be invited into the living room of each home for a homemade treat and the opportunity to have our costumes admired by the hosting neighbor. It was quite a production, filled with many wonderful memories of laughter and yummy treats.

One Halloween my family broke tradition and attended the special party hosted by the youth group at our church in the nearby town. While we were gone, some of the older neighborhood boys took advantage of our absence. We had not been home to give out treats, so we received the consequences—tricks! We came home from church to discover our front porch blasted with raw eggs and tomatoes and covered with the limbs of our willow tree that my father had trimmed the previous day. It was a mess!

My father got on the phone and talked to a few of our neighbors. It wasn't more than an hour before the culprits had been identified. The next morning, the repentant young men and their fathers appeared at our front door to clean up the previous night's mess and to apologize for their actions.

I learned that day that it was nearly impossible to get away with any mischief in our neighborhood. It was as though everyone took the words of Philippians 2:4 to heart: "Each of you should look not only to your own interests, but also to the interests of others." Everyone knew everyone else, and the adults had this unique sense of responsibility for one another and all of the children. If a 16-year-old sped down the street too fast, a caring neighbor would make a call to the parents of the offending speeder.

There was a safety net of care and concern stretched across that little neighborhood that served all of us well. As a youngster, I wasn't all that appreciative of it, but in retrospect, I see the tremendous benefit. Caring adults were always looking out for us, making certain that our growing up years were safe and enjoyable. I thank God for the care and concern I received from Mr. Twigg, Grandma McCray, May Miller, Edna Robinette, and all the others who took to heart their role as true neighbors. Our neighborhoods today should be so blessed.

Prayer: Lord, thank You for those who have safeguarded us during our growing up years—friends and neighbors who partnered with our parents in keeping an eye on our well-being and seeing that no harm came to us. Help us to be good neighbors, reflecting the love of Christ in all of our works and actions so others may come to know His love and find life in Him! Amen.

Dave Weidner

A MODEL TO FOLLOW

*When they had crossed, Elijah said to Elisha, "Tell me, what can
I do for you before I am taken from you?"
"Let me inherit a double portion of your spirit," Elisha replied.
"You have asked a difficult thing," Elijah said, "yet if you see me
when I am taken from you, it will be yours—otherwise not."
2 Kings 2:9–10*

ASSET 14: ADULT ROLE MODELS
Parent(s) and other adults model positive, responsible behavior.

It seems as though every publication I read talks about the importance of adult role models for developing healthy youth. Youth ministry publications talk about how important adult leaders are, how we should involve parents more. The cover story in the May/June 1999 issue of *Scouting Magazine* discussed the importance of adult males for the healthy emotional development of adolescent boys. Television commercials urge us to volunteer to be adult mentors to keep teens out of trouble.

America has rediscovered what many of us who live with and work with teens have known for years: We have done a serious disservice to the young people of this country by not being adult role models. For many reasons, parents voluntarily have turned over the raising of their young adults to others. In many cases, they leave a void that is filled by friends, gangs, and outsiders.

There has never been a time when being a volunteer leader for youth has been more important. We are on the front lines when it comes to being a role model for the youth in our congregations and community. I often urge the volunteers with whom I work to take the time to be involved in the lives of youth. These volunteers often are surprised at the greetings they receive from the youth when they see them in the community.

But serving as a role model for youth has its pressure. Our lives are constantly being examined by the youth with whom we live or work. The young people look for us to be consistent in what we tell them and how we act in our daily lives. They also look to us for direction that other adults in the community and sometimes their own parents are not giving them.

Being youth workers and volunteers in the church also gives us the opportunity to share our Christian values, ethics, and our faith lives with young people. God provides us numerous opportunities to share and receive His grace.

Recently a junior-high class I was leading studied the story of Elijah and Elisha. Elijah had spent years mentoring a young Elisha to be his replacement. Now the time had come for Elijah to depart the earth, and he asked Elisha an important question, "What can I do for you before I am taken from you?"

"Let me inherit a double portion of your spirit," was Elisha's reply.

Elijah realized what a difficult request this was, but he honored Elisha's choice. " 'You have asked a difficult thing,' Elijah said, 'yet if you see me when I am taken from you, it will be yours—otherwise not' " (2 Kings 2:10). As we know Elisha did witness Elijah's departure in the fiery chariot, and he did inherit a double portion of his mentor's spirit.

Now, we may not be God's prophet like Elijah, but we do have an equally important role. We have the opportunity to share our faith with the youth with whom we live or work. I am reminded of the words of the great mission hymn, "Hark, the Voice of Jesus Calling":

> *If you cannot speak like angels,*
> *If you cannot preach like Paul,*
> *You can tell the love of Jesus;*
> *You can say he died for all.*

If you cannot rouse the wicked
With the judgment's dread alarms,
You can lead the little children
To the Savior's waiting arms.
What a challenge and blessing!

Prayer: Dear Lord, thank You for giving us the opportunity to be in Your service. Help us through our daily lives to model for young people the life You have called us to live. Help us to let others see You through us. In Jesus' name. Amen.

Mark Sengele

DUCKS IN A ROW

★★★★★

Don't let anyone look down on you because you are young,
but set an example for the believers in speech, in life,
in love, in faith and in purity.
1 Timothy 4:12

ASSET 15: POSITIVE PEER INFLUENCE
Young person's best friends model responsible behavior.

The other day I was over at the pond and noticed a mother duck
and her five ducklings swimming and feeding. The mother carefully
scouted out the shoreline and the ducklings followed behind her. If I
came too close, the mother would swim toward the middle of the
pond, and the ducklings would follow to safety. What a beautiful
image—God our Father leading us as the mother duck leads her ducklings.

We've all seen them—a group of young people who dress the same,
wear their hair the same, talk the same, carry the same notebooks,
chew the same gum—like ducks in a row. There is no doubt that a
young person's best friends have a tremendous influence on his or her
behavior. What a huge impact our young people have in the world as
their faithful lives set an example for those around them. As Paul
encourages young Timothy in 1 Timothy 4:12, so we need to encourage the young people in our homes, congregations, schools and communities to be faithful examples of God's will at work in their lives.

Prayer: Lord Jesus Christ, as we live with and work with and along-
side teens, lead us to help them positively influence their
peers so by their example, others may be led to You. In
Jesus' name. Amen.

Curt Jungkuntz

Meeting Expectations

*Even youths grow tired and weary, and young men stumble and fall;
but those who hope in the LORD will renew their strength.
They will soar on wings like eagles; they will run
and not grow weary,
they will walk and not be faint.*
Isaiah 40:30–31

ASSET 16: HIGH EXPECTATIONS
Both parent(s) and teachers encourage the young person to do well.

Recently, there has been plenty of talk about self-esteem among teenagers. Self-esteem is a key factor in the future success of young people, as shown by many studies. Individuals need to recognize their self-worth before they try new things.

How do we encourage positive self-esteem? Simply praising people will not do it. (Not to mention that we are reminded each week during worship that we are, by nature, sinful and unclean. Where is the self-esteem in that?) Likewise, giving youth small and simple tasks to accomplish won't do it either.

A positive self-concept is realized when youth recognize that they are truly gifted and talented. While spiritual gifts surveys may be helpful, the proof that an individual is gifted in administration or helping or teaching comes when those skills are put into action. It doesn't always come easy. Any teacher is incredibly frightened when the first lesson is taught. Any seminarian is scared to death when he preaches his first sermon. These are big tasks—but once these high expectations are met, the result is positive growth.

Have you ever watched a young child try to climb the stairs for the first time? Certainly the task is daunting. It is truly a challenge, and success does not come without hard work. Most children will make great efforts to ascend the staircase. Finally, when the top is reached, they swell with pride.

Have you faced a challenging task? Whether it is planning an event, working on your income tax return, or running a marathon, these things do not come easy. When the goal is met, there is that satisfying feeling of success and pride. You gained self-confidence in realizing that you had the skills and abilities to complete this task.

So it is true with the teens with whom we live and work. Positive self-esteem is developed when they accomplish a goal that requires them to stretch. Just as a muscle becomes stronger when it is tested by lifting more and more weight, humans become stronger when they are stretched to meet high expectations.

As individuals who care about youth, we can encourage youth to stretch and grow—not just in their faith, but in using their gifts and abilities. Are you giving youth the opportunity to use their skills in challenging ways so they recognize all God has enabled them to do?

St. Paul writes to the Philippians, "I can do everything through Him who gives me strength" (Philippians 4:13). How can we encourage youth to examine this verse in their lives?

Imagine this situation: Youthworker Jack and his group are making plans to attend a national youth gathering. At a meeting, they complete some quick calculations to determine the funds needed for the trip. The task seems enormous—in a period of a year, the youth will need to raise thousands of dollars to pay for registration and transportation. Jack realizes he has a choice: either he can spend his year planning fundraisers (in addition to his full-time job at the bank and taking care of his family) or he can involve the youth in every step of the process.

At the meeting, Jack and the youth set a goal: to raise the funds for the gathering. Then they brainstorm fundraising ideas. Jack assigns two youth members to be the chairpersons of each event. Some youth seem shocked at the idea of being in charge of an event. "You want *me* to plan the entire spaghetti dinner? I've never even made dinner for the five members of my family!" one youth states. Jack explains that he knows they are capable of great things and that he and the other youth members are there for support.

How did things go for Jack and the youth? Certainly there were times when they were stressed and frustrated. Fundraising is not easy! Jack helped everyone to make plans, and he oversaw each event. He did not assign the task and let anyone flounder. As a result of his expectations, the youth realized they were capable of great things. Paul's words to the Philippians were put into action.

Having high expectations of our youth is an important building block for their healthy development. It sends the message that they are capable and talented. It gives them experiences that help them grow in their skills. It builds a positive self-concept as the youth see their gifts and talents put into action. It gives youth the opportunity to be the church of today.

Prayer: Lord, You have given each of us gifts and talents to use in Your church. Help us to give youth opportunities to use their gifts to do great things for Your kingdom. Amen.

Gretchen Gorline

MAKING MUSIC TOGETHER

Shout for joy to the LORD, all the earth, burst into jubilant
song with music; make music to the LORD with the harp, with the
harp and the sound of singing, with trumpets and the blast of the
ram's horn—shout for joy before the LORD, the King.
Psalm 98:4–6

ASSET 17: CREATIVE ACTIVITIES
Young person spends three or more hours per week in lessons or practice in music, theater, or other arts.

Being a part of a musical group reminds me of an image from the Bible. Like the human body, a band or a choir has many members, each with his or her own part to play. The members perform together and use their skills to create beautiful music.

Music is a great gift from God and an endeavor many, if not most, kids want to try out. I had the opportunity to attend my son's fifth-grade band concert. Normally I approach these events with a certain reluctance. After all, fifth-grade band concerts are not usually attended with any hope for real musical enjoyment. The event is held in the junior high gym, a venue complete with bleacher seats, gymnasium smells, and poor ventilation.

The previous December had brought their first concert. It displayed the power of sound: loud, blowzy, and with the bare outlines of musical form. Most of the songs were in unison with the usual squeaks, squawks, and sputters that accompany new horn players. Kids fidgeted and talked between numbers, posture was lax at best, and the dress code was apparent only if you had read the paper sent home by the band director. Nonetheless, I was impressed by how far the group had come in such a short time. One could almost imagine a miraculous transformation similar to that in the grand finale of "The Music Man," with the kids jumping out of their chairs and marching in perfect formation around the gym floor and out the gym doors.

I will have to wait a while longer for my musical miracle, but other battles had been won since that first concert. The students walked confidently to their seats and waited quietly and patiently for the director. When she raised her baton, they lifted their horns in precision. Everyone was neatly attired in the required white and black. The musicians were now playing musical arrangements that highlighted the individual instrument groups.

As I listened and watched, I had some time to reflect on what had been lost to gain this ability. Students come to formal study of music for a variety of reasons: some for glory and some because their parents sent them. The creation of sound and rhythmic noise has a primordial appeal to every child, but it is with discipline and submission of individual pleasure that we learn to harness our powers together and create music and harmony as a group. There are obvious lessons about putting away our egos and personal ambition to do it together. That "dying to oneself" in a small way mirrors the Christian's call to become a new creation through submission, though I doubt the fifth-grade saxophone section would wholeheartedly agree.

Being part of a musical group requires one to use a unique combination of senses, intuition, skill, and nonverbal communication to create a greater whole. You learn to combine your strengths with the strengths of others and to make sure that your strength doesn't overwhelm the weakness of others. The central focus is not your individual effort; rather, it is how your individual effort flows into and lifts the power of the music. This is teamwork taken to a new height. There are no cheerleaders and no coaches shouting from the sidelines. There can be no words of encouragement or disparagement from other team members. There is no opposition. There is only the object of the ideal.

Through the study of music, students begin to sense the pulse underlying the piece, the need for a reflection between stimulus and response, and the strength that comes from listening to one another breathe and breathing with one another.

There are a few more lessons ahead for the fifth-grade band. I'm sure the director would like to have a few more members who are willing to put aside the pulse of their tapping feet and adhere to her tempo, but that will come. Not all the members will continue with their studies, but everyone will remember their days in the band. You can be sure that all of them will someday be caught saying, "I used to play in the band." The power of music and the joy of making music in a group is an experience that will be part of their lives forever. Bleacher seats may always be uncomfortable. Gymnasiums will always have that certain odor. But most important, a joyful noise is always a welcome offering to God.

Prayer: Lord, help us to make joyful noise to You with our lives. May we always remember to praise You for the wonderful gift of forgiveness and eternal life in heaven that you give us through the death and resurrection of Jesus, our Savior and Lord, in whose name we pray. Amen.

Nancy Murphy

It's about Time

★★★★★

There are different kinds of gifts, but the same Spirit. There are different kinds of service, but the same Lord. There are different kinds of working, but the same God works all of them in all men. Now to each one the manifestation of the Spirit is given for the common good. To one there is given through the Spirit the message of wisdom, to another, the message of knowledge by means of the same Spirit, to another faith by the same Spirit, to another gifts of healing by that one Spirit.
1 Corinthians 12:4–8

Asset 18: Youth Programs
Young person spends three or more hours per week in sports, clubs, or organizations at school and/or in the community.

God gives us all that we are and all that we have, including our time and our talents. We, in turn, return a portion, a tithe, to God.

Why do we tithe? Why do we give something back? The Bible says when we don't, we rob God. (Check out Malachi 3:8.) Equally important is the reality that when we don't give our tithes we deprive the Lord's ministries of the resources they need to proclaim the Gospel, as well as feed, clothe, and care for God's people.

And we can remember that our tithe is not only about money. We also can tithe the time and talent with which we are blessed. We have the opportunity to help young people see their gifts of leadership and service as blessings from the Lord and things to be shared in His service. We also have the promise of God's blessings on the process. " 'Bring the whole tithe into the storehouse, that there may be food in My house. Test Me in this,' says the LORD Almighty, 'and see if I will not throw open the floodgates of heaven and pour out so much blessing that you will not have room enough for it' " (Malachi 3:10).

We can talk with teens about the stewardship of time and talents. I work with a youth board that plans annual youth gatherings in the

Chicago area. These young people are elected by their peers to serve a one-year term. During this time, there are monthly meetings, calls, and outings. The youth chosen for this board usually are outgoing and involved in many things, including sports, clubs, and groups at school, church, and in their communities. No matter how much I stress the amount of work and responsibility involved in their board commitment, it is never clear until the hard choices need to be made. When kids have to make choices about balancing and managing time and talent, there's pain and anxiety, tension, and frustration. It can be sad. A blessing from God becomes drudgery.

We want our youth to share their talents because they are gifts from God. We remember our responsibility to help nurture their gifts and to give them opportunity to use those gifts and to succeed. But when teens become overextended, the same talents and gifts that got them involved can be the things that cause them to fail.

As parents and youth workers, we can be mindful of our role in helping cultivate young people's gifts from God. I'm impressed with the amount of time and talent that youth are required to manage and how often they do a great job. But I also need to help them learn how to direct and nurture the use of these gifts. As parents and leaders, we can help youth make conscious choices so they are not caught in the situation of sharing many talents but doing nothing well. Sometimes we are afraid to challenge youth to choose. But when we are good stewards of God's gifts, we will challenge youth to make choices that will be healthy for everyone. Learning how to accomplish that may involve some pain, but it is ultimately best for everyone. And in the process, God will be glorified and His people cared for and nurtured.

The author of Ecclesiastes wrote, "There is a time for everything and a season for every activity under heaven" (3:1). As one reads through the list of times in this chapter, one is struck that nowhere does it say that these things must all happen at the same time. It's when we try to do everything that we become overextended, tense, and filled with stress and frustration. That's not God's design. That's not His plan. It's time a lot of people, adults included, learn that.

Prayer: Father, I thank You for the many gifts You've given me. I thank You for the young people You've given me to disciple. I thank You for their families who support, love, and care for them. I thank You for the many spiritual gifts You have given freely and distributed throughout our community for the strengthening and building of Your kingdom. Lord God, I ask that You would give me the faithfulness to be an example of good stewardship of my time and talents, that You would give me the wisdom to help teach Your young servants how to be good stewards of their gifts, including their time. These things I ask in Jesus' name. Amen.

Yvonne Crumpton

GOD IS NEVER BORING

*On the first day of the week we came together to break bread.
Paul spoke to the people and, because he intended to leave the next
day, kept on talking until midnight. There were many lamps in the
upstairs room where we were meeting. Seated in a window was a
young man named Eutychus, who was sinking into a deep sleep as
Paul talked on and on. When he was sound asleep,
he fell to the ground from the third story and was picked up dead.
Paul went down, threw himself on the young man and put his arms
around him. "Don't be alarmed," he said. "He's alive!"
Then he went upstairs again and broke bread and ate. After talking
until daylight, he left. The people took the young man
home alive and were greatly comforted.*
Acts 20:7–12

ASSET 19: RELIGIOUS COMMUNITY
Young person spends one or more hours per week in activities in a religious institution.

The tale of Eutychus always has been one of my favorite Bible stories, especially when it comes to youth ministry. Perhaps you've never read the story or it failed to register as a significant part of Scripture. It's not very long, and all things considered, it's not one of the more obvious stories. Perhaps, as many people approach youth ministry, Eutychus's story is one that is easily overlooked.

Eutychus was a teenager who had the wonderful opportunity to hear St. Paul speak firsthand. Eutychus and others gathered in a house. Then Paul began to speak. He seems to have been under some compulsion to cover a great deal of material. Luke tells us in Acts that Paul was going to leave the next day. He had a lot to say, so he talked "on and on" (Acts 20:9).

Eutychus was seated in an upstairs window. And the later it got and the more Paul talked, the sleepier Eutychus became. In the process, he dropped off, literally, and fell out of the window. His fellow listeners picked him up dead.

Well, you look at the story and it appears to be the worst of places Eutychus could have been and the best of places. The worst because he was killed. The best because Paul was there. Paul went to him. Embraced him. And, by the grace of God, Eutychus lived.

There's a lot of research around these days that says kids with a spiritual connection do better than those without such a connection. The research says kids that are connected to worship and religious growth are more likely to succeed.

Kids seem to know that. Most kids don't have problems with God or the miraculous. In fact, the concept of God is rather appealing. They don't reject religion or spiritual things out of hand. Indeed, they are very open to spiritual things.

Sorry to say, sometimes even the best intended church programs may get in the way. Scripture itself says that St. Paul went "on and on," which is not the way kids learn best. Eutychus became tired—that's what Scripture says—and he fell asleep. Maybe he was tired because he stayed up too late the previous night. There could be any number of reasons, including the length of Paul's talk. It's not because the Holy Spirit wasn't there. It's not because Eutychus wanted to fall asleep or that he was bored. Although the spirit may have been willing, the flesh was weak. It's not unlike the disciples in the garden with Jesus.

I'm sorry to say it, but sometimes the church does seem to put its kids to sleep. I imagine there are quite a few parents whose children have leaned over a time or two in church and said, "This is boring." For some reason, the kids haven't connected. It's not that the Gospel isn't meaningful, but for some reason the children and youth—maybe even some adults—haven't been engaged.

It becomes more problematic in a postmodern, post-Christian age. People may feel they have more options then ever, including the option to tune out on the church as irrelevant, intolerant, and disconnected. It happens even in the "best" of families. Conversations with any number of professional church workers have ended in speculation regarding the future of these church worker's children and their disinterest or disconnectedness from the church. *What will their future be? What about future grandchildren? What about heaven? Will I see my own children in heaven?*

It's a fact: Kids who are connected spiritually do better in life. Kids connected to Christ as their Lord and Savior do better *forever*. We can go on and on, but don't we sometimes have to admit that we end up putting our kids to sleep spiritually? It's a haunting question, but it's not intended to be an accusation. Rather, it is a challenge.

How do we engage our young people? Are they free to ask their questions? Do they feel attached to their church? Are there ways for them to use their energies, gifts, and talents? Are there ways for them to serve their Lord? That would certainly be God's intention.

We'll say it again. Kids who are connected spiritually do better in life. We know it. The Gospel of Jesus Christ is the way to a full life on earth and eternal life hereafter. You can't do better than that.

Kids will tell you Jesus is never boring! Never! Sorry to say, they won't always tell you the same thing about the church.

Prayer: Lord, keep us from getting in Your way. Attach Yourself to our children, and fill their lives with Your Spirit. Build their faith and faithfulness. Nourish and nurture them in Your Word and Sacrament. Use us, Lord, to share the love You pour out to us and to encourage our children in their lives with You. We don't want to lose a single young person. We want to be able to say, like Paul, "Don't be alarmed. He is alive!" (verse 10). In Jesus' name. Amen.

Terry K. Dittmer

ALONE OR LONELY

★★★★★

"Do not let your hearts be troubled. Trust in God; trust also in Me.
In My Father's house are many rooms; if it were not so,
I would have told you. I am going there to prepare a place for you.
And if I go and prepare a place for you, I will come back and
take you to be with Me that you also may be where I am."
John 14:1–3

ASSET 20: TIME AT HOME
Young person is out with friends "with nothing special to do"
two or fewer nights per week.

"I know, I know. I should spend more time at home. But I don't like it there!" Not only have I heard the words, I have lived them. Even when I was w-a-y beyond my teen years, the walls would tend to come in on me when I was by myself at home. So what do we do? We keep moving, look for distractions, turn up the music, block it out. While there are several things at work here, the question we need to deal with first is, *How do I handle aloneness?*

Do you have a certain time of the day, week, or month that you feel really alone? When we experience those times of loneliness, it is hard to believe that anyone could really understand how we feel. But there is one who has been there before us! Look at Hebrews 2:17–18: "For this reason He had to be made like His brothers in every way, in order that He might become a merciful and faithful high priest in service to God, and that He might make atonement for the sins of the people. Because He Himself suffered when He was tempted, He is able to help those who are being tempted."

Now look at Hebrews 4:15–16: "For we do not have a high priest who is unable to sympathize with our weaknesses, but we have one who has been tempted in every way, just as we are—yet was without sin. Let us then approach the throne of grace with confidence, so that we may receive mercy and find grace to help us in our time of need."

Oh yes, I can hear the "buts" already—"But Jesus was God. Tell me when He felt like I feel?" Well, let's take a look. The time was the end of Holy Week, Maundy Thursday to be exact. Sometime during that evening Jesus foretold the coming action of His disciples: "But a time is coming, and has come, when you will be scattered, each to his own home. You will leave Me all alone" (John 16:32). St. Mark writes of the fulfillment of Jesus' words in 14:50, "Then everyone deserted Him and fled."

Everyone turned their backs on Jesus—His disciples fled, His mother was silent, the crowds who once followed in admiration now had a different attitude. "Give us Barabbas! Crucify Jesus!" they shouted. Finally, while hanging on the cross, Jesus experienced the ultimate in loneliness. The Father turned His back on His own Son! "My God, My God, why have You forsaken Me?" (Matthew 27:46).

The Savior of the world was utterly alone when He paid for the sins of the world. The stabbing pains of loneliness were part of the suffering He endured for us. But equally as important to us as the fact that He suffered loneliness is the way Jesus reacted to it. His was not a response of hopelessness. Instead, He called out, "Father, into Your hands I commit My spirit" (Luke 23:46).

Yes, God the Father turned His back on His Son as Jesus hung on the cross. Jesus was totally alone, abandoned to suffer and die. Amazingly, Jesus knew this was exactly the way it must be. If people were to be saved, brought into a right relationship with God, if their sins were to be forgiven, if God's promises were to be fulfilled, this moment of aloneness must happen. If God's plan was to be completed, then Jesus knew, as God's Son, fully divine, that He would have to be abandoned, separated from His Father. Remember how Christ prayed in the garden, "Not as I will, but as You will" (Matthew 26:39).

As Jesus hung on the cross, alone, all the promises in the Old

Testament concerning who Jesus was and the truth about what was happening to Him were fulfilled. That included the promise of the resurrection.

There is a lesson here for us. God has made wonderful promises to us that hold true no matter what our condition or situation or feelings. These promises will speak to any problem we have, but let's look at them in light of loneliness. How do each of the following passages touch on loneliness?

- Matthew 28:20
- Romans 8:18, 28, 31–39
- Hebrews 13:5–6
- Philippians 4:11–13
- John 16:33

Let me give you something else to think about for the next time you feel that you have to get out of the house because the walls are closing in. Think long and hard on this statement: Everyone in the world is lonely all the time. Some simply manage to fill in the gaps a little better than others. And the root of this loneliness is not the longing for another person; it is the longing for God.

When the promise of the Lord God is in place in our lives, our loneliness can take on a new dimension—solitude. But the secret of solitude is knowing that you don't go there alone. As I sign off every letter, I now say to you: Remember, Jesus walks with you always!

Prayer: Jesus, there is a lot of loneliness in our lives. Even much of our togetherness time is not togetherness at all, but it is loneliness in the disguise of a crowd. We go out of the house to be with the gang, but the crying out for something to fill the empty spot is hardly muffled. We cruise the main drag, but we can only gawk. The party is filled with music and motion, but no one really pays attention or seems interested in the real me. Even at church, crowds seem to fill the pews, but warm greetings are mostly offered to and by the pastor. Jesus, You can fill our loneliness, changing it to solitude. And reminding us whose we are, You can make our moments of togetherness more meaningful. Make our time alone as well as with others really count for something. Touch our hearts that we may touch another's. Share Your love with us so we may share more than just time and space with others. Help us to share You as our answer to every problem and our hope for eternity. Amen.

Alan Boeck

SHIP SHAPE

*Whatever happens, conduct yourselves in a manner worthy
of the gospel of Christ. Then, whether I come and see you or only
hear about you in my absence, I will know that you stand firm in one
spirit, contending as one man for the faith of the gospel without being
frightened in any way by those who oppose you.
This is a sign to them that they will be destroyed,
but that you will be saved—and that by God.
Philippians 1:27–28*

ASSET 21: ACHIEVEMENT MOTIVATION
Young person is motivated to do well in school.

There was a young man by the name of Chip who had just received a huge job promotion in the company he had been with for the past two years. To celebrate this exciting time, he rented a sailboat to spend the weekend with three of his close friends.

The captain of the sailboat wanted Chip and his friends to be at the docks around 7 a.m. on the Saturday they were to leave. Steve, one of Chip's closest friends, rolled in about 7:30 that morning, still rubbing the sleep from his eyes. It was going to be a beautiful day with only a few clouds in the morning sky. Through the cobwebs that were still in their heads, they could sense an excitement about the day to come.

The captain gathered them together and welcomed them to his boat. "Today is a day you will not soon forget. We will see some of the most beautiful beaches known to man and water so clear that it will feel like we're swimming with the fish."

Chip and his friends began to feel the excitement of the day as they boarded the boat. "I need two volunteers," the captain said. "Good! You two will need to load the food and drinks into the boat from the dock. They are in the back of my truck over there. Take them to the lower deck. I will tell you where to put them later. Oh, don't forget the ice, it can get mighty warm out there on a day like today."

Then the captain turned to face Chip and Steve. "I'll need your help as well. There are two mops and buckets with fresh water on the other side of the boat. These decks will need to be mopped before we can leave. Start at the bow and move toward the stern. Any questions? Good!"

Chip turned to his friend and noticed that he also was picking his jaw up off the floor. "Where did you find this guy?" Steve asked. "I thought you said this was going to be a fun, relaxing weekend, not a weekend fixing up this guy's boat for him."

"I got his name from a friend at work." You could hear the tension in Chip's voice. "Said he had the time of his life on this boat."

"We ain't leaving till those decks are mopped, boys," the captain barked from inside the cabin.

Chip and Steve slowly made their way to the other side of the boat to pick up the mops and buckets. They began to mop, both of them still exhibiting disgusted looks on their faces.

About 10 minutes later, the captain showed his weather-beaten face to look at their work. "You call that mopping? A seagull does a better job with its feet than you two. You got to put your back into it and sweat a little. Start over and do it right this time."

"Chip, this guy is really chafin' my hide. Did you pay for the boat yet?" Steve asked.

"Yeah, but I guess not enough," Chip said. "Next time you see him, let me know. I have a word or two to share with him."

A few moments later, the captain poked his head out from the lower deck. Chip could hear him barking some more orders to his friends who were stocking the food and drinks. Chip, in his frustration, dropped his mop and walked over to the captain.

"Excuse me, Captain. I thought we were going to go sailing. That's what I hired you for. Why are you making us do all this work? I didn't get here at 7 in the morning to mop decks and have my friends stock your fridge."

"Okay. Everyone come here," said the captain with a frustrated tone. "Look over the front of the boat at the horizon. What do you see? Nothing? Just over that horizon is an island—an island with the whitest sand beaches you have ever seen, almost as white as snow. From a few miles off, you can begin to see the trees and the hills. As we get closer, you see the mist rising from the waterfall and begin to smell the sweet fragrance of the flowers that surround all the beaches. It isn't until we set anchor that you will notice how clear the water is and watch the fish dance with the coral."

The captain continued to cast a picture of paradise that caught the imagination of Chip and his friends. "That, my friends, is the best I can do with words to describe where we will end up today," said the captain. "But to get there, we need to do things here and now so we can enjoy the island there and then."

Chip had no problem mopping the deck after he had caught the destination. Chip could hardly wait to leave the dock and get under way. Once they finally arrived at the island, they discovered the captain was right. Words could not truly describe the island; it was more magnificent than anything they had ever seen.

Motivation to achieve is different for everyone. For some, it is no problem to wake up at 5 A.M. and jog alone. Others require continual encouragement and accountability to wake up and jog. Motivation may be a matter of knowing there is a plan and an outline for how the plan will be achieved. That's what Chip and his friends learned on their little island excursion.

Back in the Old Testament, God told the Israelites that they were about to go into captivity. They were going to be in Babylon for 70 years. But that wouldn't be the end of the story. God told them, "I know the plans I have for you ... plans to prosper you and not to harm you, plans to give you hope and a future" (Jeremiah 29:11). Motivation? Encouragement? God says to us in Ecclesiastes, "Whatever your hand finds to do, do it with all your might" (9:10).

Over the past few years, I have noticed some things about motivation. My sinful self too often pulls me into laziness and complacency. I look for shortcuts and rely on my own ways. Encouragement and accountability are what I need, and through His Word, God provides that to me in my daily life. I need to know His ways and I trust God to show me the way I should go and how to live my life. He promises His Spirit to help me, motivate me, and encourage me from one day to the next.

One blessing God gives to help in this whole process is other brothers and sisters of the faith who keep me accountable and encourage me, who share forgiveness with me and challenge me in my walk with Christ.

We rarely know exactly where we're going, and we may have only a sketchy idea about how we're going to get there, whether that's getting through school, building a successful career, starting a family, or planning for the future. What is truly good to know is God's continued presence with us. God has said, "Never will I leave you; never will I forsake you" (Hebrews 13:5).

That's motivation for a lifetime!

Prayer: Father, through the revelation of Your Word, help me to catch Your vision and the plans that You have laid out for my life. Give me encouragement, and teach me to follow You more closely. In Jesus' name. Amen.

Travis Hartjen

PREPARE TO ENGAGE

★ ★ ★ ★ ★

Pay attention and listen to the sayings of the wise;
apply your heart to what I teach.
Proverbs 22:17

Apply your heart to instruction and your ears
to words of knowledge.
Proverbs 23:12

ASSET 22: SCHOOL ENGAGEMENT
Young person is actively engaged in learning.

Brandon is a typical teenager, a sophomore, attending a Christian high school in Cleveland. He has a busy academic schedule filled with such classes as geometry, world history, German, biology, and art. Additionally, he is studying church history, in which he learns about the struggles and successes of the early apostles as they served as Jesus' witnesses "in Jerusalem, and in all Judea and Samaria, and to the ends of the earth" (Acts 1:8). He recently came to his religion teacher with a request for help.

Brandon had encountered a member of the Jehovah's Witnesses that had come in to his father's store. Unlike many people who dread the arrival of such visitors or literally hide from them, Brandon recognized his opportunity to witness his own faith. The two discussed whether Jesus Christ is truly the almighty God.

Although he did his best to explain that Jesus is Lord, Brandon felt that he was not prepared well enough for such an important conversation. Later, he and his teacher reviewed together several Scripture passages about Jesus, and they tried to get Brandon ready for an expected second visit from the Jehovah's Witness. What a powerful example Brandon is of a young person living out his faith!

It is important to note that our Lord Jesus, at age 12, engaged in discussion with teachers in the temple courts. He questioned them, listened to them, and answered their questions. May our young people be "imitators of Christ" as they learn and prepare for life in God's kingdom.

Prayer: Lord God, thank You for calling us to be Your people. Protect us from the evil of this world, and lead us to be lights so others may see our good deeds and praise our Father in heaven. Be with us, that we may be effective parents, leaders, and models of You to the young people in our lives. Inspire these young people, and enable them to boldly follow You and be witnesses for You. In the name of Jesus. Amen.

Steve Fuchs

How Many Hours a Night

Blessed is the man who finds wisdom,
the man who gains understanding,
for she is more profitable than silver
and yields better returns than gold.
Proverbs 3:13–14

Asset 23: Homework
Young person reports doing at least one hour
of homework every school day.

Have you ever stood outside a school and watched the students stream through the doors at the end of the day? It's amazing how many of them walk out, backpacks bulging with homework. I can almost imagine the phones and e-mail lines buzzing later that night. "Did you get the answer for number 10?" "I don't understand why x=3.76." "I have three chapters left. I'm staying up all night." Ah, it brings back memories.

If you polled today's teenagers, they would most likely say that homework wasn't their favorite thing to do. But when you dig deeper, many will admit there are benefits to homework. In talking with a few youth from my church, they listed the following as some of the benefits they find to be true. (Maybe your teens can add to the list themselves.)

- Ability to work in-depth on a project

- Few distractions

- Study what you need, as opposed to the needs of the class

- Challenge of doing it on your own

- Benefits of steady and gradual learning as opposed to "cramming"

- Satisfaction in accomplishment

- Good grades

Although the Bible talks quite a bit about education, we don't see any specific verses about homework. We know that Moses was an educated man, knowing the ways of the Egyptians (Acts 7:22). Solomon was known for wisdom that was reported to be as measureless as the sand on the seashore (1 Kings 4:29).

A Bible concordance lists numerous verses in the Book of Proverbs that speak of learning and wisdom. Studies of the culture in which Christ lived, which was influenced by the Greeks, show wisdom as a most-valued personality characteristic.

So what lessons can we take from Scripture regarding homework? One story that comes to mind is the parable of the three servants and their talents. A master leaves on a long journey, giving to three of his servants a measure of talents to keep for him. An accounting would take place when he returned. The first two servants used the money entrusted to them wisely and received a return for their work. The third servant was so afraid of losing the money that he hid it and awaited the master's return. When the master finally arrived, the first two servants were rewarded because they had obeyed him. The third servant was stripped of the little he had been given because it had been wasted. He also got some serious detention. (See Matthew 25:14–30 for the whole story.)

The first two servants are like those who choose to use the intellect that God gave them wisely. We see examples in our everyday lives of people who are using their brains to make our lives on earth better. It doesn't matter if it is an ambassador negotiating for peace, a scientist finding a cure for disease, or the laborer who figures out how to repair the roof. Each is using his or her God-given intellect and training to help others.

The third servant chose to hide away what the master had given. The United Negro College Fund claims, "A mind is a terrible thing to waste." Yet all around us we see those who have been given gifts and intellect wasting the time and opportunity to use them wisely. Maybe it's fear of failure, or maybe it's laziness. No matter the reason, it is wasteful.

I think that completed, well-done homework can be a reflection of our respect to God and an opportunity to use one of our most valuable gifts from Him. This Bible verse comes to mind, "So whether you eat or drink or whatever you do, do it all for the glory of God" (1 Corinthians 10:31). When we use the talents, intellect, and abilities God has given us, we show that we are the glorious crown of His creation. We never know what purpose God has in store for us or how He will use us in the future. It's great to be ready for His plan and His time.

Prayer: Creator God, You are most powerful and holy. As I look at the gifts, talents, and intellect You have given to the youth with whom I live and work, I am truly amazed! Lord, these young people are trying to learn so many things during this time in their lives. Be with them, give them strength and endurance. Help them to see the benefit of homework, and enable them to be prepared to serve You and Your kingdom, now and in the years ahead. In Jesus' name. Amen.

Dari Hartmann

HEROES LIKE US

But as for you, continue in what you have learned
and have become convinced of, because you know those
from whom you learned it.
2 Timothy 3:14

ASSET 24: BONDING TO SCHOOL
Young person cares about his or her school.

My hero is Hilbert Wiedenkeller from Franklin, Wisconsin. He was my role model. During the 1970s, "Hibby" taught music and directed the choirs at the Christian high school I attended in Milwaukee. He represented everything that was good, right, and moral at my high school. He took time for every student. He listened. He was a friend and teacher. He was my connection to the school. He was a link between what I was taught and believed at home and what was happening at school and in my life. I knew that he cared for me and demonstrated his service and love to others. I cared about my school because he cared about students and cared about his Savior. Thanks, Hibby, for everything you did for me.

How do you help young people care about their school and find a connection between school, home, and their private lives? We need to have more "heroes" in our schools, touching lives in positive and caring ways.

Today, we're at ground zero in the war: How to raise decent, healthy Christian youth when traditional ties to church, school, and community are badly frayed. Most American youth come through the critical years from ages 10 to 20 relatively unscathed. With good schools, supportive families, and caring community institutions, they grow to adulthood meeting the requirements of the workplace, the commitments to families and friends, and the responsibilities of citizenship. Even under less-than-optimal conditions for healthy growth, many of the church's youth manage to become strong Christian people and examples of Christian service to others. Some achieve this feat despite threats to their well-being that were almost unknown to their parents and grandparents, who probably experienced school as a safe haven from the outside world.

All youth have basic human needs that must be met if they are to negotiate safe passage to adulthood. Among these are the need to have caring relationships with adults, the need to receive guidance when facing sometimes overwhelming challenges, the need to be a valued member of a constructive peer group, the need to become a socially competent individual with the skills to cope successfully with everyday life, the need to believe in a promising future with real opportunities, and the need to grow in faith and love in God and service to other people.

Self-esteem and self-efficacy result from interacting positively with caring Christian adults and accomplishing tasks that help others. Care and concern come from following role models, both adult and youth, who openly demonstrate love for God and reach out to others. Youth need to hear and understand their unique qualities and special place in the plan of God.

In 1 Timothy 4:14, Paul reminds his young friend about his "gift." ("Do not neglect your gift, which was given you ...") What would happen if each Sunday school teacher, each elementary school teacher, every youth worker, and every parent honestly and openly would bring a young person into their embrace and remind them of their "gift"?

What would happen if an important role model in the life of the student would foster in the adolescent what Paul reminded Timothy of in 2 Timothy 1:6? "Fan into flame the gift of God, which is in you ... For God did not give us a spirit of timidity, but a spirit of power, of love and of self-discipline." What would happen if we had a Christian hero in every classroom and every office in our church? We do!

The impact of the adult role model can't be measured by the student's immediate reaction. At a time that glorifies their idealism and optimism and decries their hedonism and rebelliousness, we need to recognize that youth have various backgrounds, life experiences, values, and aspirations. People are unique and differ enormously in their personalities, talents, growth patterns, and coping skills. We may be planting a seed that will grow later.

A loving Christian home environment is crucial to the development of youth. Although parents remain the most significant influence on young people through the critical years, helping children mold their sense of self and shape their future life choices, adult role models in school contribute to a young person's overall connection with home.

A positive peer group also is important to youth. Although the influence of peers is often beneficial—contributing to a young person's self-esteem, sense of identity, aspirations, and achievement—the adult role model helps create a bond to caring for school and community.

Be a hero in someone's life this year. Help a young person see his unique qualities and giftedness. Take one person aside and tell her—show her—how she makes a difference in the school and church. Write a letter that congratulates a young person on an accomplishment, a word, or an idea that makes him special. Seek God's guidance in being a strong Christian hero.

It seems so simple, doesn't it? Follow the example of Christ. It's everything we were taught from a young age. Now pass the example on to others. The bond of faith that we share is held together by the power of God's Spirit and revealed in His Word.

Our schools, churches, and homes are full of heroes who make a difference in children's lives. As Paul tells Timothy: "Continue in what you have learned and have become convinced of, because you know those from whom you learned it, and how from infancy you have known the holy Scriptures, which are able to make you wise for salvation through faith in Christ Jesus" (2 Timothy 3:14).

Prayer: Dear Lord, help me to be a strong Christian role model for the young people whose lives I touch. Help me to be part of the bond that young people need to care for their school, family, and community. Allow them to grow in faith and love for Your Son, Jesus, in whose name I pray. Amen.

Ron Roma

THE BEDTIME STORY

★★★★★

Your word is a lamp to my feet and a light for my path.
Psalm 119:105

ASSET 25: READING FOR PLEASURE
Young person reads for pleasure three or more hours per week.

When I was a child, I thrived on bedtime stories. Most people probably can identify with me. I had favorite stories that were read and spoken over and over again, the words of which were my lullaby to dreamland. Mother Goose and Grimm's Fairytales. Dr. Seuss. Leo Tolstoy. (Hey, he never failed to put me to sleep in college!)

One of my favorites was a children's book adaptation of the parable of the Good Samaritan. I loved to hear the story over and over. Every time I heard it, I found myself in the parable. Sometimes I was the man beaten and robbed. Other times, I took on the skin of the Levite who was unwilling to get involved. Every once in a while, I was the Samaritan, entirely generous. Often, I saw with the eyes of the innkeeper who witnessed a great kindness. And sometimes, I was the robber, inflicting pain on the innocent. Whatever character I may have taken on, the story helped me understand how I might act in the world. I find it still defines my actions today as a citizen, a professional, a friend, a neighbor, and as a Christian.

The Search Institute's assets say that successful young people read for pleasure. I'm not sure how many kids would put reading at the top of their list of favorite things to do. Probably not a huge number. They might be willing to list magazines (lots of pictures). But right or wrong, most reading is probably assigned as homework, and by default, it is not a pleasure. It's work.

Reading expands our world. It opens the mind to all kinds of discoveries. It can stimulate the imagination and may inspire creativity. Reading gives order to our reality and defines how we act in it. It nurtures our identity. Reading helps readers experience things they may never have experienced; it can take them to places far away and introduce them to all kinds of people. Reading can delight, inform, challenge, inspire, excite. Reading brings things to life, and we can participate in that life and gain joy.

Surely this can be said of God's Word. His Word is filled with stories that catch the imagination and delight in their details. Scripture certainly informs—about sin and God's grace, about life present and eternal, about how to live today and how we shall live forever. It challenges us as it lays out God's grand design. It is filled with excitement and joy as the story of our salvation unfolds through every chapter and verse.

Perhaps one of the greatest challenges as a parent or a youth worker is to get young people to explore between the covers of their confirmation Bible. But what riches are stored there. In the Word, we discover who we are—sinner and saint, forgiven and hope-filled. In the Word, we are delighted by God's creativity, inspired by His awesomeness, overwhelmed by His generosity, motivated by His Spirit who breathes life into the reader. The details unfold to reveal how God is active in His world. The plan for living as a person of God is outlined and encouragement is offered. God's promises become promises made to each reader personally.

It is surely an asset for teens to read for pleasure. But their success is increased many times over when their reading is from God's Word. I see and I know where to go by the grace of God shown in His Word.

Prayer: Father, You have given Your people Your Word and in it stories, wisdom, guidance, and blessing for all the days of our lives. Help me in my personal engagement and study, and bless me in my efforts to show young people the joys of reading Your Word. Guide us as a lamp and light through Jesus Christ, our Lord. Amen.

Travis Scholl

THE MEINZ FAMILY DOG

★★★★★

Humble yourselves, therefore, under God's mighty hand,
that He may lift you up in due time. Cast all your anxiety
on Him because He cares for you.
1 Peter 5:6–7

ASSET 26: CARING
Young person places high value on helping other people.

Let me tell you about Moses. No, not the famous prince of Egypt. Let me tell you about the Meinz family dog—Moses. He's a purebred black Labrador retriever. We got Moses as a puppy because my wife and I wanted to practice caring for something before we had children. We figured that if we did a poor job raising a dog, he would go on Oprah in 10 years and tell the world what terrible caregivers we were. I can just hear it now...

Moses: Woof! Woof! (Translated: They never fed me! The only time I ate was when a stray cat wandered into my pen.)

Oprah: How did that make you feel?

Moses: Woof! Woof! Woof! (Loosely translated: How do you think I felt? I felt betrayed. Ignored. They didn't even care that I existed.)

Oprah: Well, Moses' owners are here. Let's bring them out.

The audience greets Amy and me with a blanket of boos and catcalls. We're humiliated and ashamed. Why did we ever get a dog in the first place?

Truth be known, we do a pretty good job taking care of Moses. We feed him twice a day, give him fresh water, walk him, run him, and play with him. We buy him treats and toys and even celebrate his birthday (August 3—send cards and presents to Walcamp Outdoor Ministries).

But caring for a dog hasn't always been easy. There were times when Amy and I were taking long trips out of state and couldn't take

Moses along. We had to line up dog-sitters, leave emergency numbers on the kitchen counter, buy enough food so the sitter wouldn't run out while we were away. Caring for something or someone who is dependent on you is not easy—but necessary.

Now that we've semi-learned how to raise a dog, we're practically veterans and children should be right around the corner. I'm sure that caring for a child is a little bit tougher though. Beyond a feeding once in a while and fresh water, I'm guessing you only have to cradle and rock the baby a couple times. Oh, there's also the small issue of changing diapers ... but after a few months, I'm told they can learn to do that themselves. Throw in a lesson about shoe tying and the birds and the bees and you've got a complete kid. If children came in a box, I'm sure the label would read "Instant Kid! Just add water." By the way—I'm just kidding.

Young people in today's society need to experience helping others in need. Jesus did in His day. Look at one of His earliest miracles.

> Jesus left the synagogue and went to the home of Simon. Simon's mother-in-law was suffering from a high fever, and they asked Jesus to help her. So He bent over her and rebuked the fever, and it left her. She got up and began to wait on them. When the sun was setting, the people brought to Jesus all who had various kinds of sickness, and laying His hands on each one, He healed them. Moreover, demons came out of many people, shouting, "You are the Son of God!" But He rebuked them and would not allow them to speak, because they knew He was the Christ. At daybreak Jesus went out to a solitary place. The people were looking for Him and when they came to where He was, they tried to keep Him from leaving them. But He said, "I must preach the good news of the kingdom of God to the other towns also, because that is why I was sent." And He kept on preaching in the synagogues of Judea. (Luke 4:38–44)

Jesus knew what it meant to care for people who needed His help. Remember when Jesus told the Pharisees in the Gospel according to Matthew: "It is not the healthy who need a doctor, but the sick. But go and learn what this means: 'I desire mercy, not sacrifice.' For I have not come to call the righteous, but sinners" (Matthew 9:12–13).

How do youth capture this same attitude? They need encouragement to do so.

I'm guessing that average or typical teenagers don't hop off the couch when they have a free afternoon and rake the neighbors yard free of charge. They usually head off to a friend's house or hang out at the mall or play on the computer. No, these aren't bad activities in and of themselves, but when the opportunity to serve arises, youth could jump at the chance. Help them find a couple who needs work done around the house or schedule a servant event at a local congregation or outdoor ministry. Maybe they could clean the youth room, baby-sit the teacher's kids, or wash the pastor's car. The possibilities are endless.

Suddenly, with the help of God, you'll see the same caring nature out of your children that we've seen and still see in Jesus. He was, is, and will continue to be the model caregiver.

Prayer: Dear Father, please provide in advance good, caring works for me to do—not because I have to, but because I want to. For I am your workmanship, created in Christ Jesus to care for others. In the name of Jesus Christ, the Savior who cared for me. Amen.

Jeff Meinz

HERE FOR A REASON

★★★★★

Read the Book of Esther

ASSET 27: EQUALITY AND SOCIAL JUSTICE
***Young person places high value on promoting equality
and reducing hunger and poverty.***

Have you ever struggled with knowing what is the right thing to do and actually carrying it out?

There was a time that I knew what I needed to do to save my people, but I was scared that I might fail.

As a young woman, I was made queen by King Xerxes. The first queen, Vashti, disobeyed a direct order of the king, which infuriated him, so he decided to get a new queen.

There were many young maidens brought to the palace when the king announced the search for a new queen. We had to go through a yearlong process before we even could be presented to the king. We were fed a special diet and had a special beauty treatment: six months with oil or myrrh and six with perfumes and cosmetics. When my time came to be presented to the king, I was nervous. But I found favor with the king, and he put a royal crown on my head and gave a banquet in my honor.

I grew accustomed to life in the palace. I was treated well by all the king's servants. I was able to see my Uncle Mordecai, who had raised me as his own after my parents died. My uncle was in good standing with the king because he had overheard an assassination plot against the king and reported it, saving the king's life.

There was one person who came to the palace that I did not care for at all. His name was Haman. He was an arrogant and pompous person. He was given a high position in the king's court and expected everyone to bow to him. My uncle wouldn't bow to him, which infuriated Haman. He decided to get even with Mordecai by destroying not only him, but our people as well. You see, I am Jewish. No one in the palace knew that. My uncle thought it would be better that way.

So Haman approached the king and told him it would be in the king's best interest to destroy a certain race of people. Without even knowing who these people were, the king told Haman to do whatever he had to do to get rid of them.

I was told by servants that my uncle was outside the courtyards, wearing sackcloth and ashes, weeping and wailing. I went to Mordecai to ask what was wrong. He told me a royal decree had been sent out announcing when the destruction of my people would take place. My uncle told me to approach the king and plead for mercy for our people. I was scared because I knew that to approach the king without his summons could mean my death, unless he extended the royal scepter to me, which meant it was okay for me to approach him.

My uncle reminded me that I could have been chosen queen for this very reason, to save my people. I told Mordecai to gather all the Jews in Susa and fast for me. I asked them not to eat or drink for three days and nights. I said that my servants and I would do the same thing. After the fast, I would go to the king, even though it was against the law. I wasn't afraid to die.

Those three days were long, but I put my trust in the Lord, who had placed me in this situation for such a time as this. I went to the king, and he allowed me to enter. I am pleased to tell you that all went well. I exposed the evil Haman and his wicked plot, and the king did not have my people destroyed.

You have, no doubt, recognized the story of Esther. But what can we learn from the story of this beautiful young woman? First, we see that some people will seek to destroy others simply because of prejudice. Second, we see that we have a choice when it comes to perpetuating prejudice. Esther could have ignored the situation (no one in the palace knew she was Jewish) and her life could have been spared. But Esther chose not to ignore the situation, and she willingly risked her life to save the lives of others.

God worked through this situation to save His people from destruction. How can God use you? God places us where we are for a reason. He gives us all that we need to face many different situations. Look around you. Are people hungry, homeless, hurting, mistreated, etc? How can God work through you to make these situations better? Are you willing to be like Esther and risk whatever it takes to make sure those around you have what they need?

Prayer: Dear heavenly Father, we thank You for the mercy and grace You give to us each and every day. We pray that You would open our eyes to the needs of the people around us. Give us the courage to do the right thing, even if it means sacrifice on our part. Lord, we ask for Your forgiveness when we fail to do the right thing, and we ask for another opportunity so You might use us to accomplish Your purpose. In the precious name of Jesus we ask these things. Amen.

Jimella Moorhead

WALKIN' THE TALK

★★★★★

It has given me great joy to find some of your
children walking in the truth, just as the Father commanded us.
2 John 4

ASSET 28: INTEGRITY
Young person acts on convictions and stands up for his or her beliefs.

The music swells. The sanctuary breaks forth with the sound of singing. You begin your victory march, walking down the aisle, your crown sparkling with each flash of the cameras. The assembly rises in adulation; every eye is focused on you. Your term as a congregational youth worker has begun!

Congratulations! Although your installation rite was probably not filled with all the pomp and celebration of a major beauty pageant, your position is by no means less important. You see, you, too, have been awarded an awesome opportunity, given a tremendous privilege, called to a position of great influence. Throughout the coming months, the ears and eyes of many will be focused in your direction. They will be listening intently to your platform: those things you value and hold dear. And they will be watching—oh, will they be watching— observing your every action and reaction to see whether you live what you profess, whether you walk your talk.

Your position demands integrity because it defines integrity for those who observe you!

The teen years are a period when issues of identity become primary. As they journey toward adulthood, the struggle of many teens is to figure out not only who they are, but who they want to be. No longer are they content to accept the "do as I say but not as I do" arguments of their younger days. Rather, they strive to incorporate values that go beyond mere idealistic dreams to heartfelt, life-altering realities. They value integrity, where belief drives action.

Sadly, models of true integrity are sorely lacking in today's society. The Scriptures, however, are full of individuals whose lives reflect this Godly characteristic. Perhaps the most outstanding models, apart from our Lord Himself, are the three men who faced death in a fiery furnace for their beliefs and the queen who risked losing her position and her life for the sake of what she valued. Let's take a moment to look at these examples.

In the Book of Daniel, we are introduced to three young Israelite noblemen who were taken into captivity by the Babylonian king, Nebuchadnezzar. While in Babylon, they were trained for three years in all the ways of their captors so they might give their allegiance to the king. But they were men of integrity.

The Babylonians altered the surroundings of these young men, tried to influence their diet, and even changed their names, but they could not change their belief in or their allegiance to the God of Israel. When the king ordered all in the land to worship his image of gold or burn, these God-fearing men refused to compromise their faith. They held to their beliefs and maintained their integrity.

In fact, in the face of their trial, they not only stood their ground, but they made a tremendous profession of faith: "If we are thrown into the blazing furnace the God we serve is able to save us from it, and He will rescue us from your hand, O king. But even if He does not, we want you to know, O king, that we will not serve your gods or worship the image of gold you have set up" (Daniel 3:17–18).

The anger of Nebuchadnezzar was kindled against Shadrach, Meshach, and Abednego. They were bound and thrown into the blazing furnace for their beliefs—and the God of their convictions went in right along with them! He protected them from the flames, ultimately delivering them unsinged, unharmed, and without even as much as the smell of fire on them! God be praised! And He was. After their deliverance from the flames, Nebuchadnezzar noted their integrity and praised their God before his entire country, acknowledging the sovereign power to save of the God of Shadrach, Meshach, and Abednego.

That's how it is with people of integrity. The stands they take often are observed and their beliefs amply noted by those inside and outside the family of faith. For the Christian, this is a witness we can neither minimize nor ignore. In fact, it is a value we can lift up and model to the generations that follow, young people who daily are confronted with their own trials by fire: pressure from peers to participate in behavior that is less than God-pleasing; pressure from the school to surrender the things of faith to scientific "fact"; pressure from society to embrace diversity of thought and abandon absolutes. The list goes on and on. And that is where your role as parent or youth worker begins to take on the importance we referred to earlier.

In the Book of Esther, a secret plot is laid to exterminate the Jewish people from the Persian Empire. Mordecai, uncle of Queen Esther, hears of the plot and pleads with the queen to intervene with the king to save her people. This was no small request. For the queen to approach the king without being summoned was against the law. It meant certain death unless the king opted to spare her life. The dilemma was huge: The potential cost to the Jews was great, but the personal cost weighed heavily on the queen's mind as well. Finally, after being reminded by her uncle of who she really was, Esther was persuaded to stand for her people—to hold fast to that which she valued as most important. The Jews—and the queen—escaped extermination.

Esther's uncle asked her to consider one thing as she weighed her predicament: "Who knows but that you have come to royal position for such a time as this?" he said (Esther 4:14). And that is the precise question we consider when dealing with the issue of integrity. Who knows but that God, in His wisdom, has chosen you to make a stand at this time, in this place, so His name might be lifted up and His power made known. Certainly, the costs can be high for such a stand, but God, who knows all about paying a price, says it's worth it! "Be faithful, even to the point of death, and I will give you the crown of life" (Revelation 2:10).

Prayer: Father, You have given us lips to speak Your praise and to testify to Your love and power. Equip us with Your Spirit so we might journey through this world as people of integrity, unafraid to take a stand for the truth. We ask this in the name of Your Son, who stood for truth in the face of all adversity and secured our victory and our great reward. Amen.

Mike Thurau

THE BEST POLICY

*Dear children, do not let anyone lead you astray. He who does
what is right is righteous, just as He is righteous. He who does what
is sinful is of the devil, because the devil has been sinning
from the beginning. The reason the Son of God appeared
was to destroy the devil's work. No one who is born of God will
continue to sin, because God's seed remains in Him; He cannot go
on sinning, because He has been born of God. This is how we know
who the children of God are and who the children of the devil are:
Anyone who does not do what is right is not a child of God; nor is
anyone who does not love his brother.*
1 John 3:7–10

ASSET 29: HONESTY
Young person tells the truth even when it is not easy.

*Why tell the truth? What does it really matter? It only matters if we get
caught, right? I wouldn't want to hurt anyone with the truth.* Do these
comments sound familiar? I have heard them from more than a few
people myself. To be honest, I'd have to admit that I have thought
them myself.

One movie that always pops in my mind when I hear the word *honest* is *Liar Liar* with Jim Carrey. For those who have never seen the
movie, a boy makes a wish for his dad to be honest with him because
his father has let him down one too many times. As a result, Jim Carrey
finds things coming out of his mouth that he thinks but has always
found another way of saying. Many people are offended. Many people
get mad at him. But he is being honest, or is he? Many of us probably
would have tried to use a little more tact in our statements while still
being honest.

One mother recently told me her child had been walking around
the house struggling to keep her mouth tightly closed. When asked
what she was doing, the child responded, "You said to keep my mouth

closed if I couldn't think of a kind way to talk. I really have something important to say but I don't know how to say it kindly."

The mother burst into laughter and responded, "If it is that important, you can talk to me honestly." Both were relieved when the air had been cleared.

Many times we ask kids to be honest with us, but we don't want to hear what they are going to tell us. Kids want us to be honest with them, yet we sugarcoat or even avoid a subject. How would the world be different if everyone were "brutally honest" with each other?

I find it extremely difficult to tell a parent when their kid is in trouble or involved in drugs, alcohol, smoking, or premarital sex. I encourage youth to be honest with their parents and for parents to be supportive rather than judgmental. But sometimes, to protect a youth, it takes someone from the outside to intervene.

Why? I often ask this question myself. The answer that I always come back to is because I care and so does God. He is using me to work in a situation or in someone's life. How can I best represent Him? God calls us to the truth over and over in the Bible.

When I looked up *truth* in my Bible concordance, I was amazed at how many times the word is used. "I am the way and the truth and the life" (John 14:6) has more meaning to me now as an adult than it ever did as a kid. One thing I always have admired in someone is the ability to tell the truth even though it may make the person look bad or admit a wrong.

I myself still find it challenging to own up to a sin and ask forgiveness. But what better model could we exhibit to the next generation? God's grace is larger than any wrong we could ever do. Why, then, do we continually hide the truth? Cover up our sins? Blame someone else? Won't our punishment be larger in the end than the small consequences we may encounter as a result of being honest with ourselves, with one another, and ultimately with God?

I find it a constant challenge to be the model God would have me to be. I find it difficult not to sugarcoat things and to find the courage to be honest with someone even though I know it will hurt the other person. It is really difficult for kids to be honest, but it is one of the most important survival skills we can teach them.

Prayer: Dear God, help me always to speak honestly with the young people in my life. Help them to see that honesty is truly what You desire for us. In Jesus' name. Amen.

Mary Lightbody

FREE TO BE RESPONSIBLE

★★★★★

*Humility and the fear of the LORD bring
wealth and honor and life. Train a child in the way he should go,
and when he is old he will not turn from it.*
Proverbs 22:4, 6

ASSET 30: RESPONSIBILITY
Young person accepts and takes personal responsibility.

Many parents, teachers, and youth leaders are looking for ways to develop joyful, productive, and responsible teens. As someone who touches young people with the love of Christ, you have a great opportunity to develop these qualities in young men and women.

The Bible says to "train a child in the way he should go, and when he is old he will not turn from it" (Proverbs 22:6). In today's complex and rapidly changing world, it is difficult to develop such qualities. But with a healthy, open, and loving relationship with your youth, you can help them grow and learn to be responsible young men and women.

The hardest thing about teaching responsibility is letting young people make their own mistakes and deal with the consequences. When Adam and Eve made the wrong choice, God allowed them to suffer the consequences. Although He did not approve of their disobedience, God loved them enough to let them make a decision and live with the results.

Remember when David sinned against God with Bathsheba? In Psalm 51, David asks forgiveness. "Have mercy on me, O God, according to Your unfailing love; according to Your great compassion blot out my transgressions. Wash away all my iniquity and cleanse me from my sin. For I know my transgressions, and my sin is always before me. Against You, You only, have I sinned and done what is evil in Your sight, so that You are proved right when You speak and justified when You judge"(51:1–4).But it did not end there. David had to deal with the consequences of his sin.

Just as David and Adam and Eve had to take responsibility for their sins, so must we. We also need to teach this to the youth in our lives. We need to understand that to take responsibility for one's action; one must have a choice in the action taken.

If a youth has a problem or does something wrong, it is our first instinct to solve the problem or to give punishment. To develop responsible young men and women, we can give youth choices about what to do. "How are you going to solve this problem?" is the question we can ask. And we can ask the question with concern and love.

We need to allow youth the privilege of solving their own problems. When we intrude into their problems, we make their problems our problems. Youth who know their problems are the concerns of adults don't worry about them. There is no need.

We need to let young people deal with the consequences of their actions. We can find loving ways to allow consequences—not adults—to teach youth. We can focus on the learning that is taking place rather than the end result. However, there are times when adults need to intervene in the problems of youth, such as when physical or spiritual harm can come to them or to others around them.

In producing responsible youth, we can love them enough to allow them to fail, love them enough to allow the consequences of their actions to teach them about responsibility, and love them enough to help them celebrate the triumphs. A young person's responsibility will grow each time he or she survives the decision-making process. May God bless your journey as you continue to see Him operate in your daily life.

Prayer: Dear heavenly gracious Father, we ask You to be with the youth of Your church and the people who strive to spread Your Word to them. We ask You to give parents and youth leaders courage, wisdom, and endurance to give the unconditional love that youth seek. And God, as we strive to teach responsibility to young people, we ask You continually to remind us of what it means to be a responsible Christian and to serve You in our daily life. We ask all of this in Your Son's most precious and holy name. Amen.

Cheryl Wilkie

HOLD BACK

Do you not know that your body is a temple of the Holy Spirit,
who is in you, whom you have received from God?
You are not your own; you were bought at a price.
Therefore honor God with your body.
1 Corinthians 6:19–20

ASSET 31: RESTRAINT
Young person believes it is important not to be sexually
active or to use alcohol or other drugs.

Recently, I was approached by a fellow youth worker to speak with a youth group member about the direction in which her relationship with her boyfriend appeared to be headed.

I was a little uneasy about the whole thing because the topic of sex before marriage was something I had never spoken about to anyone. Sure, I had been on the receiving end of the discussion with my parents, but I had never been the one to advise someone else. I felt as though this were a huge responsibility. The whole thing weighed heavy on my heart. What do I say? Where do I start?

I prayed about the situation daily, asking for guidance and wisdom. I tried to find the right place and the right time to bring up the topic. Finally, I was prepared for the big talk. We had a retreat coming up that would present the perfect opportunity. After we arrived at the retreat center and I reviewed the schedule, I found the perfect time. Then my fellow youth worker told me the situation had been taken care of and the young woman had been spoken to about the topic. I didn't know if I should be relieved or disappointed. I had really worked myself up about this, and now it was too late.

That sounds terrible: "It was too late." I had only missed the opportunity for the talk, but what if I had been too late and no one had talked to this girl? She could have ended up pregnant. Then I would have felt awful. I had pondered and procrastinated way too long. What was I thinking? It seemed to me that I had been thinking of myself and how this whole issue made me feel. As a youth worker, I shouldn't have been thinking about myself but about the two youth who were important to me.

I believe God has a plan for everything that happens in my life, so I know there was a reason I didn't have that conversation. I think God wanted me to learn to be prepared at *all* times and to be armed with Scripture to teach and guide the youth with whom I work, no matter what the issue may be. So I have equipped myself with some Scripture passages regarding the importance of the internal asset of restraint. I pray that they will help you.

Young people are surrounded by advertisements and movies that do not support restraint from sexual relationships outside marriage or the use of drugs and alcohol. In fact, I feel as though the whole sex issue is portrayed as the norm. Who isn't having sex before marriage?

In 1 Thessalonians 4, Paul tells us how important it is to live a life pleasing to God. Verse 7 says: "For God did not call us to be impure, but to live a holy life." Paul was writing about sexual immorality, but this also applies to drugs and alcohol—impurities that harm our bodies physically. Paul says in verse 8 that anyone who rejects these instructions is rejecting God. I believe that would really hit home for young people today. It's pretty cut and dried.

Another verse I have found to encourage young people is from 1 Corinthians 6. Verse 19 says that our body is a temple of the Holy Spirit, whom we have received from God. It is not our own. Verse 20 completes the thought: "You were bought at a price. Therefore honor God with your body." When young people believe it is important to restrain from sex, drugs, and alcohol, they honor God. We need to let them know that and praise them for it.

Finally, a fine example to share with young people is the story of a young man named Joseph. In Genesis 39, we read about Potiphar's wife and her desire for Joseph to sleep with her. Joseph denied her numerous times, telling her in verse 9, "How then could I do such a wicked thing and sin against God?"

Joseph knows what is right and displays great integrity when confronted with this temptation. Isn't it interesting that in his restraint, he displays another positive value—integrity? And despite his restraint and integrity, Joseph still ends up in jail because Potiphar's wife lies. But the Lord was still with Joseph and continued to show him kindness, even in prison (Genesis 39:21).

I pray that you continue to encourage the youth with whom you live or work to do what is right and honor God with their bodies as they restrain from the impurities of sex, drugs, and alcohol. How great it is that God will continue to be with them and bless them in their positive choices.

Prayer: Father, thank You for Your Word, the Bible. Help me to use it as a guide to show young people today the blessing You will give them in restraint. Help me to equip them with the wisdom and guidance they will need when they are tempted. Thank You for Your presence in their lives. In Jesus' name. Amen.

Anne Marie Hartman

BOMBS AWAY

"For I know the plans I have for you," declares the LORD,
"plans to prosper you and not to harm you, plans to give
you hope and a future."
Jeremiah 29:11

ASSET 32: PLANNING AND DECISION MAKING
Young person knows how to plan ahead and make choices.

Bruce had big plans for his future. He had just finished a very successful junior high career at the Christian grade school. Now he was preparing for the big jump into Crepe High, the only high school in his small town of 1,500 people. Like most new freshmen, he was a bit nervous about attending a new school, but because he knew all the kids in town, it was no big deal.

The one thing that excited him most about high school was the football team. In a small school like Crepe High, Bruce had no doubt that he would be the starting quarterback on the JV team. Coach Riley assured him that if he worked hard he might even make the varsity team his sophomore year. With Kim cheering him on—she was his junior high sweetheart and sure to be a JV cheerleader—he was a shoo-in!

It seemed everything was going Bruce's way—when out of the blue, his dad dropped the big bomb. "Hey, son, I've got great plans for our family. We're moving! You're going to be going to the biggest and best high school in the state!"

Am I supposed to be excited about that? Bruce thought. "So I'm supposed to pick up and leave everything I know? Why don't you just rip my heart out, Dad?" Bruce said, a bit perturbed. "Who do you think you are anyway? Just because you got a promotion and a big salary increase doesn't mean you have to change a person's whole life! Everything doesn't revolve around you!"

Have you had the "big bomb" dropped on you? Have you felt as though you've been asked to pick up and move from your comfort zone to a place that is different and maybe a bit scary or uncomfortable? Bruce had to move from his comfort zone. In that place were many things that gave him a sense of security and happiness—things such as a small high school, a girlfriend, a spot on the football team, and the confidence in his own perfect plan.

Where do you get your sense of security? As Christians, we face a daily struggle over that very question. It's an ongoing battle with the devil, the world, and our sinful flesh. The devil wants to convince us that we are in charge of our own destiny, that if you don't have a perfect plan set in motion, you're a guaranteed failure. The devil loves to accuse us as he points us to the things of this world as a road map to a perfect plan—things such as popularity, prestige, and our own talents and abilities. Then when these things let us down or are taken away from us, we're left hurting and angry, scared and alone—sometimes we even blame God.

Well, I've got good news. Your heavenly Father has a plan for you! He's known about this plan since the beginning of time. It's far better than anything you could ever dream up on your own. It's a perfect life plan, full of prosperity and security, a plan you can depend on for now and for your future! It is as sure as the plan of salvation revealed to us through Jesus Christ, God's only Son. The plan begins at the cross of Calvary, and it's been given to you as a free gift within the waters of Baptism.

Rest assured that your heavenly Father has your best interests at heart as you plan the next days, weeks, and years of your life. Keep your eyes focused on the cross of Christ as you struggle with the daily decisions you face. Thank Him for the many people He has placed in your life who support you, such as parents, pastors, teachers, and friends. Continue to test the advice given from them against the all-knowing wisdom of God found in His Word. Pray that the Holy Spirit will lead you to God-pleasing choices. When you do make that selfish and prideful choice, the promises found in God's Word and Sacrament are yours for the keeping! Praise the Lord!

Prayer: Thank You, heavenly Father, that Your wisdom is so much greater than mine. Forgive me for the times I look to other things for my security and happiness. Continue to open my eyes to the wonderful plan that You have for my life. In Jesus' name. Amen.

Nick Malleos

DECEIVED

Read Genesis 25:19–33:20

ASSET 33: INTERPERSONAL COMPETENCE
Young person has empathy, sensitivity and friendship skills.

You'll have to pardon my nervousness today. You see, I am about to be reunited with my twin brother, Esau.

We haven't seen each other in 20 years. We didn't part on the best of terms. In fact, I wouldn't be surprised if he still wanted to kill me.

You're probably wondering what I did. Let me tell you, it was bad. I am a liar, cheater, deceiver, and an opportunist. It's taken me 20 years to realize this. Of course, I had some help from God.

You've probably heard about my family. My grandfather is Abraham, and my father is Isaac. By the way, my name is Jacob. I am the second-born son. Before Esau and I were even born, God told my mother, Rebekah, that the second-born son would rule over the first-born. For whatever reason, my mother and I foolishly decided that God needed help in accomplishing His will.

One day when he was hungry, I was able to get Esau to sell me his birthright for a bowl of stew. Then my mother and I deceived my father into believing that I was my brother so he would give me the blessing. All went according to plan, but we paid a big price for our deception. My father found out I lied, I had to leave my family, and I did not trust that God's will would prevail.

During the past 20 years, God has helped me to work on my attitude. He introduced me to my Uncle Laban, who is a deceiver, liar, cheater, and an opportunist. Does this sound familiar!?!

I will never forget the first time I saw Rachel. She was incredibly beautiful—how I loved her. I agreed to work for my Uncle Laban for seven years for Rachel's hand in marriage. Those seven years passed so quickly, and soon the day that I was to wed my beloved Rachel arrived.

Imagine my surprise the day after the wedding ceremony when I found out that I was wed to Leah instead of Rachel. Of course, I was furious and demanded an explanation for this outrage! My uncle gave me some lame excuse about the eldest daughter needing to be married before the younger daughter could be married. He generously offered to let me marry Rachel after my week with Leah was up, if I would work for him for another seven years. I had no choice. I loved Rachel, so I agreed.

I, the deceiver, had been deceived by another. I realized for the first time how my brother and father must have felt after my mother and I deceived them. I had been so self-absorbed, only thinking about what I wanted. Never once did I stop to think about the impact my actions would have on my family. What a painful way to learn that every decision we make concerning ourselves has an impact on others.

I also have seen how my Uncle Laban's deception has hurt his daughters' relationship with each other. I fell in love with Rachel. She's the woman of my dreams. I know this hurts Leah terribly, but I certainly didn't plan for our marriage to happen. I wonder if my Uncle Laban realizes the price his daughters have paid for his lies.

My heart goes out to Leah. She tries so hard to be a good wife. God has heard her crying and has blessed her with many fine sons for me. Rachel is jealous because we have had only one child together. Remember this, everything you do affects others either directly or indirectly.

It is getting closer to the time that I will see my brother. I have sent many gifts on ahead. When I see him, I will greet him with the respect and honor that he deserves. I only hope that he will forgive me for what I have done. Maybe he will give me a chance to tell him what I have told you.

Thanks for listening to what I had to say. Before I leave, I would like to pray with you.

Prayer: Dear Lord, You are so gracious and merciful to us in our sinfulness. Thank You for Your forgiveness and patience as You work with us through Your Spirit. Remind us that You don't need our interference to accomplish the plan You have for our lives. Help us humbly to come before You, seeking Your guidance and direction. We pray that we would look at others with the eyes of Christ, seeing others the way You see them. We also ask in the precious name of Jesus for the strength to be the kind of Christian friend You would have us be. Amen.

Jimella Moorhead

My World Is Different

★★★★★

This is what the LORD Almighty says: "Administer true justice;
show mercy and compassion to one another. Do not oppress
the widow or the fatherless, the alien or the poor.
In your hearts, do not think evil of each other."
Zechariah 7:9–10

ASSET 34: CULTURAL COMPETENCE
Young person has knowledge of and comfort with
people of different cultural/racial/ethnic backgrounds.

As you think about your dealings with youth, ask yourself the following questions: Am I an example to youth and others when it comes to zero tolerance for exclusivity? Do I model welcoming the stranger? Who is the stranger in my life? In my church?

Sometimes we are so comfortable in our long-standing relationships and comfort zones that we forget we are called to be welcoming to the stranger. The stranger comes in many different accents, physical abilities, complexions, and dialects. It is so easy to be intolerant of those whom we do not know or understand.

I was at a luncheon meeting of a group called CUSP, which works to create intentional partnerships between urban and suburban culturally different congregations. All but two of the 16 people were strangers to me. They happened to come from different church denominations, which in itself can be a culture shock. For this group to work, it was decided we needed to get to know one another. At the close of the meeting, we were directed to participate in a reconciliation exercise. The facilitator of the exercise gave us the following directions.

He asked us to form a circle with arms around one another. We all joined in this rainbow circle of faces—a circle of strangers. A voice said, "Being a part of a group can be encouraging because we can enjoy the feeling of togetherness, a sense of community. But it doesn't always work that way, and sometimes the group becomes a clique." A pause of silence.

"Sometimes we separate ourselves from each other and cannot enjoy the love God intends for us," the facilitator said, followed by a short pause. "If you have been a part of a group and have ever let the group down, drop your arms to your side." All arms dropped. A pause.

"Sometimes we say things that are harmful about individuals or groups of people. Anyone who's ever said something harmful to/about an individual or spoken in a derogatory way of another group of people take a step backward." To my surprise, everyone stepped backward. Short pause.

"Often we exclude individuals or whole classes of people from our group." Pause. "If anyone has ever excluded another person or class of people from the group or made someone feel left out, whether it was because of race, economics, looks, or anything, please take a step backward." Again, to my surprise, everyone stepped backward!

"Sometimes we say things that aren't true or speak half-truths and even fail to speak up. We deny making mistakes or admit we're unwilling or afraid to speak up in defense of someone. If this has happened to you, I'd like you to turn and face away from the center of the circle." Everyone turned!

He continued, "Sometimes we pretend not to see the needs of other people. We knowingly and unknowingly isolate and insulate ourselves from those in need. If there have been times you've ignored the needs of others and remained apart from them, close your eyes and keep them closed."

Then he said, "We're meant to be together, yet at times our actions keep us apart." A short pause. "If you have ever helped someone with a need, turn around."

"It's important to listen to people." A pause. "If you have ever taken time to listen to a friend who had a problem or tried to understand a different group of people, hearing their issues, take one step in."

"We build up people when we welcome them and make them feel included." A short pause. "If you've ever made someone feel welcome and a part of things, especially someone of another culture or economic group, open your eyes." Everyone had his or her eyes open.

The leader continued, "Confession to one another can tear down walls." A pause. "If you've ever shared a way that you failed someone or admitted your prejudices, take another step in." Everyone stepped in!

The leader concluded, "God asks us to forgive one another." A short pause. "If you've ever forgiven someone, place your arms around the people beside you. Amen." Surprised, we were all back where we had started—in a circle of faces, embracing one another. The difference this time was that we were no longer strangers. We all knew there was much we had in common because we did this seven-minute exercise.

The young person who has knowledge of and comfort with people of different cultural, racial, or ethnic backgrounds already knows that it is a learning process to accept the stranger. Am I a model of this? Have I been a model for the young people whose lives I touch?

The amazing lesson I learned from this exercise was that we all are very much alike while being very different. We can model and teach that it is our Christian responsibility not to allow anyone to feel like a stranger. Two young men wreaked havoc on their school in Columbine, Colorado. I suspect in many ways they felt like unwelcome strangers. They were strangers at school to their classmates and teachers. They were strangers at home to their parents and neighbors. If we work to help youth become tolerant and welcoming to the stranger, we might stop another suicide or school massacre.

Although the above sentiment may be true, consider a couple other

Gospel truths. One is from St. Paul: "For all have sinned and fall short of the glory of God, and are justified freely by His grace through the redemption that came by Christ Jesus" (Romans 3:23–24). Also consider: "This is good and pleases God our Savior, who wants all men to be saved and to come to a knowledge of the truth" (1 Timothy 2:3).

In this postmodern, post-Christian world, the acceptance of strangers most often means acceptance of alternative lifestyles, theologies, spiritualities, and creeds, no matter how alien they may be to us as God's people. Remember that all people are sinners. God calls us to love the sinners, but not the sin. I can accept the diversity that fills our earth, but I need to take care not to accommodate deviance from God's Word in the process. I may embrace the stranger without adopting alien concepts contrary to my Christian faith.

God will use me as an instrument for bringing others to Himself. I can remember that part of being an accepting friend is to share the Gospel of Jesus Christ, my true and best friend, who gave his life on the cross for all people. Apart from God's truth, there can be no true unity. Without Jesus, there cannot be true reconciliation or peace or community.

Prayer: Gracious and loving Father, be my guide as I work to be an instrument of Your peace. Help me to be a devoted servant and to do justice. Direct my path to be understanding and to show love to those who are not quite like me. Order my steps as I feed the hungry and clothe the naked. In Jesus' name. Amen.

Yvonne Crumpton

MORE THAN A MOTOWN REVIEW!

★★★★★

Read Luke 4:1–13

ASSET 35: RESISTANCE SKILLS
*Young person can resist negative peer pressure
and dangerous situations.*

It was a beautiful day, the kind one wants to spend outdoors. Warm breezes brought the smell of clean, fresh air filled with the fragrance of newly opened blooms. A woman walked through the lush garden, admiring the beautiful, abundant flowers. As she stooped to pick a few blossoms, she noticed a "Do Not Pick the Flowers" sign among the blooms. While tempted, she walked on to take in other joys of the day.

A modern Eve? What if Eve had paid attention to the "Do Not" sign posted on the Tree of Knowledge? What if temptation would have been resisted? What if the devil had failed in his attempt to plunder the good in the garden? Temptation was the downfall of man. The signs are all around us even today: "Thou shall not…" "Don't do that" "You shouldn't…" Yet we still give in to temptation.

Temptation—to be offered something that is forbidden or unwise for some reason, to lay the choices before a person. Temptation may be blatant or subtle. Satan seeks our souls subtly, persistently, and pushes at our most vulnerable spots. Had Eve resisted the temptation at the Tree of Knowledge, the devil would have sought another way to try her soul.

Eve chose not to resist temptation. So did Adam, Cain, King David, Peter, and the Rich Man. Jonah knew what he ought to do, but he didn't do it. Paul put it succinctly (if not a bit intricately) in Romans 7:15–20: "I do not understand what I do. For what I want to do I do not do, but what I hate I do. And if I do what I do not want to do, I agree that the law is good. As it is, it is no longer I myself who do it, but it is sin living in me. I know that nothing good lives in me, that is, in my sinful nature. For I have the desire to do what is good, but I cannot carry it out. For what I do is not the good I want to do; no, the evil I do not want to do—this I keep on doing. No, if I do what I do not want to do, it is no longer I who do it, but it is sin living in me that does it."

Satan, the master of deception, knows our weaknesses and lays the most tempting choices before us. What is your temptation: sex, money, shopping, food, love, gambling, lies, alcohol, tobacco, drugs, over-work? No one is immune to it.

Imagine if Eve had refused the devil. The dialogue may have been:

"No thanks, snake. I've been told not to eat that."

To which Satan replies, "Ah, now a little bite won't hurt anything."

"No," Eve reiterates a bit more forcefully.

Satan takes a more subtle track. "But who does God think He is to tell You, His favorite creation, what to do and not to do? Didn't He put you in charge of everything?"

"What part of no don't you understand?!?" Eve asks.

What would Satan's next move have been? More deception? A different tactic? A new target? Why is it so difficult to resist? The devil is a persistent, intelligent enemy, and our flesh is weak!

Being able to resist the devil requires discipline—spiritual discipline—in a society that promotes not getting caught and lack of consequences when someone does get caught. Spiritual discipline means understanding and acting on the boundaries of what Jesus would have us do to live out our faith. Resistance means deciphering what to say no to and when to say it. Consider the model of resistance Jesus demonstrated in Luke 4:1–13.

1. Know the Scriptures. Satan knows them and twists the words to his purpose. Jesus answered temptation with the truth.

2. Respect the boundaries God has placed on Christian living. Our

body is a temple of the Holy Spirit; keep it clean and healthy physically, mentally, relationally, and spiritually.

3. Apply the trouble rule: Will this get me into trouble with anyone in authority? With anyone who is significant to me? With God? Respond faithfully.

Resisting temptation is difficult, and far more complex than just saying no. The world offers many choices, and the devil makes them all the more tempting, knowing what pushes our hot buttons as well as our pleasure sensors.

The Christian life is not about trying to pattern one's behavior after Jesus and doing good works. Rather, the Christian life we lead is about trusting in what Christ has done for us. To be sure, God's Law is clear enough and sets forth what God would have us do. But Jesus is not just another Law-giver; He is the Law-Fulfiller. Therein lies the reason we can resist temptation, or as the apostle John wrote: "My dear children, I write this to you so that you will not sin. But if anybody does sin, we have one who speaks to the Father in our defense—Jesus Christ, the Righteous One" (1 John 2:1).

Prayer: Lord Jesus Christ, I put my trust in You and rely on Your embrace. I know You will never let me go. Enable me, by Your grace, to resist temptation, and protect me from the evil one. Help me in my contacts with young people to help them see what You have done for them to keep us all a part of Your kingdom. In Your name I pray. Amen.

Marilyn Bader

Too Late for Tommy

★★★★★

A man's wisdom gives him patience; it is to
his glory to overlook an offense.
Proverbs 19:11

Asset 36: Peaceful Conflict Resolutions
Young person seeks to resolve conflict nonviolently.

Seventeen-year-old Tom stood alone in his parent's darkened garage. His father's shotgun positioned in his mouth, Tom's tears stained the long steel barrel.

"I'm sick of arguing with you, Tommy! Don't ever call me again. I never want to see you for the rest of my life!"

His girlfriend, Brenda, had phoned him an hour before with that news. They had been fighting about the course of their relationship for what seemed like weeks. Brenda had finally decided she wanted out of the whole mess. Dumping Tom seemed to be the best alternative to her.

Tom was hopelessly in love with Brenda. He felt life was not worth living if she wasn't in it. His finger quivered on the trigger. "She'll be sorry. I can't face the thought of not being with her. I can't stand the pain. I'm sick of the fighting."

Tom wanted escape from the conflict. Escape from the pain. The shotgun seemed to be the best solution for a no-win situation. He closed his eyes, said "I'm sorry," and pulled the trigger.

It was hours later when that garage door finally opened as Tom's mom drove up the driveway from work. She found her son lying in a large pool of dark blood, the shotgun nearby. In shock, she dialed 911.

The ambulance hadn't even arrived at Tom's home when the phone began to ring. Thinking it might be her husband, Tom's mother rushed to answer it.

"Is Tom there?" It was Brenda. All she heard was uncontrollable crying on the other end of the line. "Tommy is that you?" Brenda asked. "I'm really sorry for what I said to you. I've had a change of heart. Let's get back together, okay?"

"This isn't Tommy," his mom said through her tears. "He shot himself. I just called 911."

"Oh!" Brenda blurted out. "I'm so, so, sorry. I was calling to apologize."

Tom's mother slowly hung up the phone. Reconciliation came too late for Tommy.

This story is true, though the names have been changed. And, unfortunately, stories like this continue to be played out every day in America. In fact, suicide is the number two killer of our young people.

Conflict often catches teens, like all of us, off guard. Sometimes we say or do things we later regret. When we are hurt or offended, we may react without thinking. It's a natural reaction.

How do you typically respond to conflict or offense by others? Is it to react with force or intimidation? Is your response a verbal attack, gossip, or slander? Some people in our world resort to physical violence. And, in extreme cases, the response to unresolved conflict could even lead to murder or, in Tom's case, suicide.

In the Book of Proverbs, it says that "a man's wisdom gives him patience; it is to his glory to overlook an offense" (19:11). Patience is such a difficult virtue to obtain. We all seem to want it yesterday! But patience, according to God's Word, comes from wisdom. And this true and Godly wisdom comes for life experience, the making of mistakes and learning from them.

Wisdom is a gift given by God. It comes from the daily rhythm of God's Law and Gospel operative in our lives. The daily ebb and flow of confession and absolution. The recognition of our sinfulness and the celebration of God's love and forgiveness given to us freely, by God's grace, through faith in Jesus Christ.

It is truly the wise person who can be patient with others. That hasty word, that rash decision, jumping to the wrong conclusions, or making a faulty assumption has started wars, ended marriages, and ruined friendships. Had the person only been a little more patient, waited a little longer—the outcome may have been so very different. It certainly would have in Tom's case. He still would be alive today.

Search Institute has identified "peaceful conflict resolution," namely, "a young person's ability to seek to resolve conflict nonviolently," as an important asset that all of us should strive to develop. Not surprisingly, bookstores are full of courses, books, and advice on how to solve conflict in a peaceful way. But for the most part, these formulas and methods tend to be so much pious advice and law-oriented in approach.

To truly live out Proverbs 19:11—to have the wisdom necessary to be patient with one another and to overlook someone's offenses—requires a trip to Calvary. It requires standing beneath the crucified body of Jesus Christ and seeing firsthand the forbearance of the Father toward His people. It requires seeing the Wisdom of God impaled on the wood. It requires understanding and appreciating that God can overlook our offenses because He placed them on His only begotten Son in our stead so we might be forgiven.

People will offend us. It is inevitable. As someone once said, "Where two or three are gathered in Jesus' name, there eventually will be conflict." Yes, it even happens in the Church and among God's people.

But we have the greatest power for peaceful conflict resolution in that same Church where we so often see conflict. We have the true Wisdom—the wisdom the world cannot give. And we have the promise of God to grant us the strength to overlook offenses against us as we beseech the Holy Spirit to mold us in the image of Jesus. Blessed are the peacemakers because they will be called the sons of God.

Prayer: Father, we are sinners. And sinners cause conflict and react to it with even more sin. Forgive us for the sake of Your Son, Jesus, who was the mediator between You and us. By Your Holy Spirit, we pray that You would give us the wisdom and the patience to overlook offenses made against us. And that turning the other cheek in forgiveness, we might thereby give glory to You and testimony to our faith in Your Son, in whose name we pray. Amen.

Jeffery S. Schubert

A Matter of Adoption

★★★★★

Read Galatians 3:26–4:7 and John 8:31–36

Asset 37: Personal Power
Young person feels he or she has control over "things that happen to me."

Sean at first thought that it would be great to have a dad again when his mom announced she was going to remarry. His new stepfather said it would be great to have a young man to take fishing and to ball games. With only Sean and his mom these last few years, the thought of someone else in the household caused some anxiety, but the opportunity to do "guy things" mom did not enjoy and to have a "dad" like most of the other kids in his second-grade class seemed to hold a whole new world of promise and good times.

Well, that was more than five years ago, and Bill, Sean's stepdad, had proven not only to be a disappointment in not keeping his promises, but Sean had grown to live in fear of his temper and what seemed to be unreasonable and unpredictable expectations. To top it off, there were now two younger half brothers that Bill seemed to favor so much more because they were "his own." Those boys could sure seem to get Sean in trouble when he had to baby-sit, which was almost all the time because his mom worked now.

Sean attended a huge urban school where many of his friends told stories of experiences in the world. To a young man, now 14 and in the eighth grade, Sean felt he would never have any of those experiences. It felt as though his life was always under somebody else's control. He felt powerless; he felt as though nobody wanted his opinion. Did anyone care what he thought? Would he ever have the opportunity to show he could make good decisions? He thought he wanted freedom, but he really wanted to feel he had some choice in what happened to him.

One morning when Sean got up for school, it was cold and overcast, which seemed to fit the mood of the apartment. Mom told him to dress nicely; he was not going to school. They were going downtown as a family.

"Why?" Sean asked.

"You'll find out, dear," was her cryptic reply. Again, no choice, no idea, of what was to happen.

"I'd really rather go to school," Sean said. School was actually a better place than home these days. A teacher Sean liked made life there feel good. As a good student, Sean felt some control over what happened and he felt that teachers valued him. As an eighth-grader, he often was picked to do volunteer tasks that took him out of the classroom and sometimes placed him in charge of younger kids who liked him and looked up to him. That seemed more preferable to a day with his mom, Bill, and his brothers at an unknown place.

"We have something important to do as a family," his mother replied. "Get dressed. Wear a tie, okay?"

Several hours later in a crowded elevator headed for the ninth floor of the Family Court Building, it became clear what was happening. "When we step before the judge, explain how you care for the boy and politely explain your desire for the family to have one name. Then I will continue with the adoption proceedings. Any questions? Good!" the man in the suit told Bill.

So that was it! They were going to change his last name to Bill's! When was he supposed to find out? Would anybody like to know his opinion? Did anyone care? Sean froze. The bell rang, the door opened, and the stranger said, "This is us." In a daze, Sean had to be told to exit the elevator.

It all went as planned—by others. The judge listened, mom spoke, Bill spoke, the lawyer spoke. Finally, the judge asked Sean if he wanted the new name. This was the moment to speak, say it, say no, but the fear of repercussions at home, the anger of his stepdad, the tears of his mom, and the pattern of abuse and put-downs and powerlessness was too strong. "It's okay, sir," was all Sean could say.

"Very well. Done. Next case."

Throughout adolescence and into his 20s, Sean carried the name he grew to resent as a symbol of his powerlessness, of the fact that others controlled his life. One makes adjustments. We can learn to live with many things—even if they are not good for us—but the consequences can be evil. As a teen Sean left home and had terrible things happen in a desperate bid for some choice and control in his life. He said he wanted freedom. He wanted some control over what was happening around him.

But through his struggles, Sean experienced the grace of God, and somehow (Sean says miraculously) God guided Sean to a healthy place as an adult. Sean now looks back at his life and sees how God's power moved through his life. At times when Sean felt the least powerful, he now sees how God helped him make it through. He can say with St. Paul, "That is why for Christ's sake, I delight in weaknesses, in insults, in hardships, in persecutions, in difficulties. For when I am weak, then I am strong" (2 Corinthians 12:10).

Now Sean is a teacher and a youth worker at his church. He makes every effort to help young people understand the choices they have, the consequences of those choices, and to develop the wisdom to make good choices. He wants people to know the Gospel can free them from power struggles and control issues in their relationships and offer healing now and forever. He is known as a good listener and makes every effort to help parents and youth listen to each other, value each other's opinions, and connect and explain how they got here—and where they are going.

The term "personal power," as the Search Institute's assets use it, is language of the law. If "personal power" as Sean and Bill understood it is only about control, then we always will be lost in the law and we always will struggle in darkness with one another over who is in control. Ultimately the sense of powerlessness will never go away as long as it's dependent on our own efforts.

But when our "personal power" grows from the understanding of our adoption as heirs of the Gospel—as gifted in Jesus by faith in Him, His death, and resurrection—then we are given real freedom to experience security that allows us to value the thoughts and feelings of others and to ask their opinions without feeling threatened. Then it's not a matter of control. It is, rather, that we are secure in the love of Christ who knows our weakness and loves us as we are into eternity.

Prayer: Lord Jesus, by Your walk to the cross, by Your vulnerability to suffering and death, You have shown the meaning of true power, a life of service secure in the Father's love. By Your Spirit help us to lead lives that empower young people to make choices pleasing to You and a blessing to them. Amen.

Harry Therwanger

CHRIST, MY SOURCE

★★★★★

May our Lord Jesus Christ Himself and God our Father,
who loved us and by His grace gave us eternal
encouragement and good hope, encourage your hearts
and strengthen you in every good deed and word.
2 Thessalonians 2:16–17

ASSET 38: SELF-ESTEEM
Young person reports having a high self-esteem.

What are youth thinking when they say they have a high self-esteem? Do they really believe they are valuable to God, their family, friends, and community?

As the oldest of three children, I grew up being a part of family meetings. Here our voices were heard and our opinions counted, not that we had the final say. My parents were raised during the generation in which "children were to be seen and not heard," which is not what they wanted for our family. In fact, Sundays in our house were family days. We went to church, then did a family outing. Oh, how I remember the Sunday afternoon drives! As a youth I dreaded them because I really was not interested in being driven around to look at houses. Now I cherish and value the time we spent together.

My self-esteem was nurtured by my family, and as a youth, I knew I was valuable to them. That didn't keep me from comparing myself to my friends, though, and it seemed I was never quite up to par with "certain" others. I couldn't be the fastest on the team or always get the best grade, so I struggled with my self-image. After hearing Bible verses such as "I am fearfully and wonderfully made" (Psalm 139:14), I started thinking, *Are my zits fearful and the rest of me wonderful? What does this really mean?* Praise God that while man looks at the outward appearance, God looks at the heart (1 Samuel 16:7). My parents' gentle guidance and reassurance told me who I was on the inside was the most important.

Knowing we are living in the image of Jesus does not come naturally. "Train a child in the way he should go, and when he is old he will not turn from it" (Proverbs 22:6). As adults we are given the responsibility to train children and youth. So what do I know? I am a youth worker. I struggle with my own self-image, so who am I to train others? What can I do to assist youth in seeing themselves as valuable without encouraging in them the same false conceit with which I struggle? I am glad I am not alone in feeling these inadequacies. Moses thought he was slow of speech and tongue. Even after God's assurance, he didn't want to commit himself to the job of leading the Israelites.

Many kids are looking for a sense of who they are and what they are worth. Ultimately, it's like shooting in the wind. No matter how much you tell teens they are worth something, there are going to be times of failure when they feel like total zeros. Then self-esteem, no matter how high and lofty sounding a concept it may be, comes up vacant and empty. And the teen remains lost.

Who and what we are truly comes from what Jesus Christ has done for us. God loved us, each one, so much that He gave His own Son to die for us so we could be adopted into His family. He welcomes us with His strong embrace. And He would have done it for any one of us, even if we were the only one in need of saving. Remember that passage from Timothy? "God wants *all* to be saved" (1 Timothy 2:4). That's how much you are worth to God.

Now God has put you and me, as people who care for and work with youth, in a position of training. He gives us our life experiences to share with the youth we know. Through our faith walk, and in our personal story to youth about our own inadequacies, we are living examples to the strength of Jesus in our lives. Jesus walks with us in our trials, and it is especially in these times that we develop realistic opinions of ourselves and see our failures. We can share these weaknesses with our youth so together we all can rejoice in the grace we have through Jesus and give praise and thanks to Him! The best way to live is to let them see Christ as our source of strength.

> I have been crucified with Christ and I no longer live, but Christ lives in me. The life I live in the body, I live by faith in the Son of God who loved me and gave Himself for me. (Galatians 2:20)

Prayer: Dear Lord, without You I am nothing. Thank You for Your unending love. Please give me the courage and strength to share my weaknesses and boldly proclaim Your strength to the youth You have put into my charge. It is through You that I can do all things! Amen.

Mary Oldenburg

SENSE OF PURPOSE

*If you have any encouragement from being united with Christ,
if any comfort from His love, if any fellowship with the Spirit,
if any tenderness and compassion, then make my joy complete by being
like-minded, having the same love, being one in spirit and purpose.
Do nothing out of selfish ambition or vain conceit, but in humility
consider others better than yourselves. Each of you should look not only
to your own interests, but also to the interests of others. Your attitude
should be the same as that of Christ Jesus.*
Philippians 2:1–5

ASSET 39: SENSE OF PURPOSE
Young person reports that "my life has a purpose."

For any of us who have changed majors in college or lost a job, the difficulty of finding one's purpose in life is easily understood. We need to find out who we are and who we are meant to be so we can plan our next moves. We consider our interests and, if we are Christian and alert, we consider what direction God might have planned for our lives (Galatians 1:10).

We know God created us, but for what purpose? God redeemed us in Baptism, cleaning up our identity as heirs, but what are we to do? Should we look our best? Be "successful"? Serve God? How?

We are the result of God's actions of love. Philippians 2:1–5 gives us insight. We are to have the same love, spirit, and purpose of Christ, considering others better than ourselves. We are to look not only to our interests, but also to the interests of others. We can have Jesus' attitude; after all, we are His body, the Church. Jesus can use our bodies to continue His healing, loving touch and to spread the message of new life in Him. Every single one of us is an important part of Jesus' body! (Read Romans 12, which summarizes this very well.) We will not want to abuse our bodies or end this life if we keep this purpose in mind.

But what if God's will conflicts with ours? Remember Paul when he was Saul, persecuting the Jews (Acts 22:3–13)? What he was doing was anything but God's will. But God gave Paul a new sense of purpose, a new direction. Later Paul would write, "It is God who works in you to will and to act according to His good purpose" (Philippians 2:13).

Galatians 4:18 reads: "It is fine to be zealous, provided the purpose is good." God persuaded Paul to change his will to God's will. When our will is matched to God's will, then the promise is ours: "In all things God works for the good of those who love Him, who have been called according to His purpose" (Romans 8:28). We are reminded whose we are and, therefore, what we are asked to do. We love God and are called for His purposes.

So what is this good purpose? How do we choose our goals? "Love God and obey His commands," says 1 John 5:3. If God's will conflicts with ours, our purpose will be thwarted (Psalm 3:10). So we can acknowledge what God is doing in our lives (Proverbs 3:6), give thanks in all things (1 Thessalonians 5:18), and wait on the Lord until our direction is apparent (Hosea 12:6). For example, our family did that when we met 2-year-old Lois after applying for adoption. The adoption worker told us we could give her back in a month if it didn't seem to be working out. The first month was very difficult with biting and sleepless nights for all because of Lois's singing. We only could base our decision on our trust that God had led us to her as we had asked Him to do. We could not go by how things felt. We trusted God's purpose and promise that all things work together for good. And we still do to this day—eight years later!

In this time of personal mission statements, we make our purposes agree with God's. And we can help others by encouraging them to listen to God, in addition to giving them our counsel. This is loving our neighbors as ourselves (Luke 10:27). We may not know what God is doing and we do not want to regret having frustrated God's purposes.

God promises help in Hebrews 13:21 and 2 Timothy 3:16–17. God equips us for every good work. Daily repentance and cleansing renew our openness to follow God's path each minute of our lives. And in following, we have peace beyond understanding!

Prayer: Lord of all creation, forgive us for making choices without Your blessing. Thank You for redeeming our lives and giving us the purpose of passing on Your love to all around us. Equip us by making our will match Your purpose. In Jesus' name. Amen.

Eunice McKinney

JOSEPH'S BONES ARE BURIED IN THE PROMISED LAND

★★★★★

And Joseph's bones, which the Israelites had brought up from Egypt,
were buried at Shechem in the tract of land that Jacob bought for a
hundred pieces of silver from the sons of Hamor, the father of
Shechem. This became the inheritance of Joseph's descendants.
Joshua 24:32

ASSET 40: POSITIVE VIEW OF PERSONAL FUTURE
Young person is optimistic about his or her personal future.

In the entire human history of the world, if anyone has had a positive view of their personal future, it is Joseph, the favorite son of Jacob, the son of Isaac, the son of Abraham, the father of faith.

Joseph was, of course, the second youngest son of 12 in Jacob's family and the first child of Rachel. Because Rachel was the woman whom Jacob loved with all his heart, Joseph was the son Jacob loved above all others.

I guess that's where a positive view of a personal future begins—in the precious, deep, abiding love of parents. It often takes too much to overcome the negativity of abuse, confusion, and heartbreak that occurs in children's lives when mom and dad make it clear from the beginning that they are unwanted. The future becomes despair.

But I digress.

Joseph's positive view of his personal future begins with Jacob's love, and that future had a symbol. Joseph's future was bright because he wore a coat of rainbow colors. But his positive future became truly promising when he began to hear Yahweh, the God of promises. Early on, Yahweh made it abundantly clear to Joseph that his future was not only bright, it was phenomenal. So Joseph, believing his home was a completely safe environment, took joy in telling his mother, his father, and his 11 brothers of his dreams, his visions, and the great promises that were gifts to him from God.

Joseph assumed too much. His family home was not completely safe. What Joseph considered good news to be shared and celebrated was interpreted by his brothers as arrogance and conceit.

Joseph's rainbow coat was soon covered in blood. His own brothers threw him into a well—into the heart of darkness—and left him for dead. As far as Joseph's brothers knew, they had murdered their own brother.

But then they changed their minds. The brothers decided to make a profit on Joseph's life. They sold him into slavery in Egypt. They lied to Jacob, staging Joseph's death.

In Egypt, Joseph became the most trusted servant of a powerful man, but he was framed and thrown in jail for refusing to have sex with his master's wife. Hard to stay positive when you're in chains for a crime you didn't commit, when moral integrity lands you behind bars.

Despite the injustice and misfortune and all the pain inflicted beyond his control, Joseph's perspective did not change. He remained steadfast, always listening to God. And Joseph's divine revelations gave him position with Pharaoh, and Pharaoh gave him charge of all Egypt.

But Joseph went further. He believed the unbelievable. He trusted that the future would reconcile his brothers to him—the same brothers who had been bent on his destruction. More amazing, Joseph believed he would see his father again.

That's why Joseph cried when he beheld his brother Benjamin in Egypt (Genesis 43:29–30). These were tears of the deepest joy—Joseph saw God's promises fulfilled before his very eyes. Yahweh consummated the possibility of reconciliation, transforming a physical famine into a spiritual harvest. God's greatest gift to Joseph was the capacity to forgive a nearly unforgivable crime. (Read for yourself the moving account of Joseph's reconciliation with his brothers in Genesis 45:1–28. No storyteller can do justice to the graceful drama written there.)

Joseph trusted the promises of Yahweh. Yahweh counted that trust as righteousness so no matter what happened, Joseph's future was more than positive, it was *promising*.

For that faith, for that persevering trust, Joseph's bones were buried in the Promised Land, long after he had died, by the nation of a promise.

So what does this mean for us?

Ultimately, we know that a positive view of a personal future is rooted in faith in God's promises. His promises give us *hope*.

Undoubtedly, you know young people who have no reason to hope. Their lives have been shattered by the selfish wills of people who should love them selflessly. They are angry and cynical, depressed and confused. At some point in your life, you may have known their despair.

But you know the promises of God. Articulate them every way you can. Share them with every young life you have the privilege to touch. Tell Joseph's story. For our bones, too, shall one day be buried in the Promised Land.

Prayer: Father, we trust in Your promises. Keep faith vibrant in our hearts until the day our bones see the Promised Land. We pray through Your Son, whose life hammered to a cross, then resurrected, gives us the life to enjoy Your gifts. Amen.

Travis Scholl

Assets for Developing Healthy Teens

Identified by Search Institute, Inc.

Asset 1: Family Support
Family life provides high levels of love and support.

Asset 2: Positive Family Communication
Young person and his or her parent(s) communicate positively, and young person is willing to seek advice and counsel from parent(s).

Asset 3: Other Adult Relationships
Young person receives support from three or more non-parent adults.

Asset 4: Caring Neighborhood
Young person experiences caring neighbors.

Asset 5: Caring School Climate
School provides a caring, encouraging environment.

Asset 6: Parent Involvement in Schooling
Parent(s) are actively involved in helping young person succeed in school.

Asset 7: Community Values Youth
Young person perceives that adults in the community value youth.

Asset 8: Youth as Resources
Young person is given useful roles in the community.

Asset 9: Service to Others
Young person serves in the community one hour or more per week.

Asset 10: Safety
Young person feels safe at home, school, and in the neighborhood.

Asset 11: Family Boundaries
Family has clear rules and consequences and monitors the young person's whereabouts.

Asset 12: School Boundaries
School provides clear rules and consequences.

Asset 13: Neighborhood Boundaries
Neighbors take responsibility for monitoring young person's behavior.

Asset 14: Adult Role Models
Parent(s) and other adults model positive, responsible behavior.

Asset 15: Positive Peer Influence
Young person's best friends model responsible behavior.

Asset 16: High Expectations
Both parent(s) and teachers encourage the young person to do well.

Asset 17: Creative Activities
Young person spends three or more hours per week in lessons or practice in music, theater, or other arts.

Asset 18: Youth Programs
Young person spends three or more hours per week in sports, clubs, or organizations at school and/or in the community.

Asset 19: Religious Community
Young person spends one or more hours per week in activities in a religious institution.

Asset 20: Time at Home
Young person is out with friends "with nothing special to do" two or fewer nights per week.

Asset 21: Achievement Motivation
Young person is motivated to do well in school.

Asset 22: School Engagement
Young person is actively engaged in learning.

Asset 23: Homework
Young person reports doing at least one hour of homework every school day.

Asset 24: Bonding to School
Young person cares about his or her school.

Asset 25: Reading for Pleasure
Young person reads for pleasure three or more hours per week.

Asset 26: Caring
Young person places high value on helping other people.

Asset 27: Equality and Social Justice
Young person places high value on promoting equality and reducing hunger and poverty.

Asset 28: Integrity
Young person acts on convictions and stands up for his or her beliefs.

Asset 29: Honesty
Young person tells the truth even when it is not easy.

Asset 30: Responsibility
Young person accepts and takes personal responsibility.

Asset 31: Restraint
Young person believes it is important not to be sexually active or to use alcohol or other drugs.

Asset 32: Planning and Decision Making
Young person knows how to plan ahead and make choices.

Asset 33: Interpersonal Competence
Young person has empathy, sensitivity and friendship skills.

Asset 34: Cultural Competence
Young person has knowledge of and comfort with people of different cultural/racial/ethnic backgrounds.

Asset 35: Resistance Skills
Young person can resist negative peer pressure and dangerous situations.

Asset 36: Peaceful Conflict Resolutions
Young person seeks to resolve conflict nonviolently.

Asset 37: Personal Power
Young person feels he or she has control over "things that happen to me."

Asset 38: Self-Esteem
Young person reports having a high self-esteem.

Asset 39: Sense of Purpose
Young person reports that "my life has a purpose."

Asset 40: Positive View of Personal Future
Young person is optimistic about his or her personal future.